HONK!

Andy Buck with Rob Gibbons,
Oliver Caviglioli and Fergal Roche

JOHN
CATT

First Published 2019

by John Catt Educational Ltd,
15 Riduna Park, Station Road,
Melton, Woodbridge IP12 1QT

Tel: +44 (0) 1394 389850
Email: enquiries@johncatt.com
Website: www.johncatt.com

ISBN: 978 1 912906 17 8

Set and designed by John Catt Educational Limited

Our emerging workforce is not interested in command-and-control leadership. They don't want to do things because I said so; they want to do things because they want to do them.

IRENE ROSENFELD
CEO, Mondel

Contents

About the contributors

ANDY BUCK

Best-selling author, speaker, trainer and coach, Andy started his working life as a teacher and headteacher. His subsequent career has included leading an organisation with over 8,000 employees, working as a senior civil servant and founding three successful start-up businesses. His passion is unlocking potential in others through inspiring and effective leadership. He is also slightly obsessed with geese.

ROB GIBBONS

Rob started out as an importer, wholesaler and retailer, running a successful operation with his partners for over 20 years. Now he's making his mark developing two new businesses: Silver Australia in Melbourne and Innoscent Skincare in Bangkok. He combines this with his passion for people development through sports management and coaching. His goal is to bring fresh thinking to the table, gained from his years of travelling and observing different cultures at work and play.

FERGAL ROCHE

One of the leading education entrepreneurs in the UK, Fergal set up and developed The Key, which achieved a 50% market share in a decade and is now regarded as the must-have digital support service for anyone running a school. It has featured in the *Sunday Times Fast Track 100* and has won a number of sector awards. Fergal ran three schools, was business development director of a FTSE 100 company, strategy director for a $4bn international privately-held company, and was once-upon-a-time training to be a Jesuit priest. He failed dramatically in at least two of those ventures.

OLIVER CAVIGLIOLI

Oliver was a special school headteacher for a decade before becoming a trainer and author of several books on visual teaching strategies. The son of an architect, Oliver fuses his home design education with his passion for cognitive science to produce a variety of visuals that communicate insights from research for busy professionals.

Foreword

Great Britain's women's hockey team winning the gold medal in the 2016 Olympics was, for me, one of the most exciting sporting moments of recent years. It was the goal-keeper, Maddie Hinch, who stole our hearts with her extraordinary performance in the penalty shootout.

WhatsApp achieved a valuation of $19bn in 2014, when it only had 55 employees. That's about $350m per employee. Today, it has 1.5 billion users and sees 60 billion messages sent per day.

So what? Well, both are examples of extraordinary human performance through teamwork.

And organisations are basically just teams, or collections of teams.

Leading teams is one of the most enterprising and exhilarating activities on the planet. Doing it well impacts positively on the lives of so many people. And doing it badly? Well, you don't need me to tell you about that. But just ask one of the members of the GB hockey team or WhatsApp what it was like to be part of their team. Tough, crazy hard work, disciplined … and brilliant.

Over an eleven-year period, I had the privilege of leading my company, The Key, through various modes of existence. In 2007 we were a startup team funded by government, housed within a digital concierge company. At the end of 2008 we had an email from the government giving us three months' notice to shut down. We negotiated our way into leasing the brand from the Department for Education and getting schools to pay for what had originally been a free service. It took three years before our income was outstripping our costs. It took another year to turn The Key into a company in its own right, and then find an investor who would fund me and my management team to become independent from the digital concierge company, the Ten Group. Then we had to learn how to work with private equity investors controlling a board where I had previously had pretty much free rein. Somehow we managed, and by 2018 we had nearly 50% of schools in England and Wales paying an annual subscription, with surveys showing that our customers were more likely to recommend us to others than just about any other brand out there, including the likes of Apple and John Lewis. Quite a journey, which is now continuing without me.

Organisations that do well don't just get lucky. They learn disciplines; they understand and monitor their environment; they watch their competitors like hawks; they climb inside their customers' brains to discover what is driving their behaviour; and they orient their products and services around the needs of those customers. They get information that is produced in as close to real time as possible so they can see how effective they are being. For example, if you are a professional rugby player, data from the monitor on your chest will be scrutinised by the coaches at every moment of the match and decisions are made accordingly as to how much longer to keep you on the pitch. This kind of information is the lifeblood of any organisation and keeps it highly tuned, like a fine engine.

I have three kids and I tell them to consider how they might like to end up leading a business or an organisation and how intellectually and morally satisfying this can be. Intellectually, because finding the right balance in all the different elements that come into play demands huge brain power, and morally, because you have the opportunity to make a big difference to the world around you, especially in how you treat your co-workers.

So, enjoy your read and reflect deeply as you go. I think you'll find this a profoundly human journey, where the emphasis is on being real and humble. You don't have to be a genius to do well, but you do have to get the best out of others. Phil Knight gave way to an eccentric member of his team when he agreed to name his company Nike. Other colleagues told Phil that his own idea, *Dimension Six*, was terrible, and he eventually demurred, as great leaders do. I love that humble, but ultimately very wise attitude, which characterises the very best organisations around us.

Enjoy the book and enjoy your journey. May you find success and significance as you go.

Fergal Roche
Founding CEO, The Key, 2007-2018

Understand your leadership balance

The challenge of leadership is to be strong, but not rude; be kind, but not weak; be bold, but not bully; be thoughtful, but not lazy; be humble, but not timid; be proud, but not arrogant; have humour but without folly.

JIM ROHN
American entrepreneur, author and motivational speaker.

We'd better explain about the geese and why this book is called *Honk!*

According to an article published in the journal *Science* in 1970, when geese fly in formation it improves their aerodynamic efficiency by around 70%. Over the years, this work has spawned all sorts of other claims about geese and lessons we can learn about leadership. Whatever the validity of some of these claims, they provide an elegant metaphor for the power of shared goals, effective teamwork and successful delivery in any personal or business endeavour.

Geese flying in formation 'honk' to encourage those up front to keep up the pace

FIVE LEADERSHIP LESSONS FROM GEESE

LESSON 1 – THE IMPORTANCE OF ACHIEVING GOALS

As each goose flaps its wings it creates an uplift for the birds that follow. By flying in a 'V' formation the whole flock adds 71% extra to the flying range. When we have a sense of community and focus, we create trust and can help each other to achieve our goals.

LESSON 2 – THE IMPORTANCE OF TEAMWORK

When a goose falls out of formation it suddenly feels the drag and resistance of flying alone. It quickly moves back to take advantage of the lifting power of the birds in front. If we had as much sense as geese, we would stay in formation with those headed where we want to go. We would be willing to accept their help and give our help to others.

LESSON 3 – THE IMPORTANCE OF SHARING

When a goose tires of flying up front it drops back into formation and another goose flies to the point position. It pays to take turns doing the hard tasks. We should respect and protect each other's unique arrangement of skills, capabilities, talents and resources.

LESSON 4 – THE IMPORTANCE OF EMPATHY AND UNDERSTANDING

When a goose gets sick, two geese drop out of formation and follow it down to the ground to help and protect it. If we had as much sense as geese, we would stand by each other in difficult times, as well as when we are strong.

LESSON 5 – THE IMPORTANCE OF ENCOURAGEMENT

Geese flying in formation 'honk' to encourage those up front to keep up the pace. We need to make sure our honking is encouraging. In groups and teams where there is encouragement, production is much greater.

The final leadership lesson is of course the inspiration for the title of our book. Whether you are working on strategy, building relationships in your team or just getting stuff done, the power of keeping things positive runs through everything we believe. Even having tough conversations, while sometimes hard, is in the end about making a positive difference for your colleagues and your organisation.

This book focuses on what great leadership looks like at all levels, both within organisations and beyond them. It unashamedly aims to cover leadership in a huge range of contexts. As a leader reading this, you may be at the beginning of your leadership journey, taking your very first steps into leadership within an organisation. Or you may be the CEO responsible for the entire organisation. Or anything in between.

What really matters is the leadership balance you create

We have found that while the focus of your work as a leader will undoubtedly shift according to your role, many of the key elements of great leadership are present at every level and in every setting, regardless of your experience or sphere of influence. All that differs is your context, and to say otherwise, in our view, is to over-complicate the issue. Great leadership is the same, however senior you happen to be. What matters is how you apply your understanding of the situation to enable you to focus your leadership actions and approach to suit your context. And what really matters is the leadership balance you create.

For example, if you are a brand-new head of sales and marketing in a small start-up, you need to quickly assess the capacity of the team delivering this important work before deciding what the team needs to do next. You also need to consider how you should approach making this change happen. If capacity and expertise is low, the right approach may very well be quite directive. On the other hand, if the team is more experienced and highly competent, such an approach is likely to backfire. This is no different if you are the CEO taking over a company and working out what the strategic priorities need to be over the next three to five years and how best to implement them. The only difference is the scale.

Our work has given us a privileged insight into hundreds of organisations

So, the approach of this book is to take a hard look at what great leadership looks like and allow you to translate this into your own context and create the right leadership balance for you and your team. Our own experience has shown us the power of this approach, where our work has given us a privileged insight into hundreds of organisations. Where leaders create a shared set of values, goals and ways of working, there is no limit to what is possible, so long as leaders at all levels keep a good leadership balance and can take their agreed shared approaches and modify them to suit their situation. It is also worth remembering that the more you can think of your organisation's leadership capacity existing at all levels within the staff team, the better. All leaders in an organisation can feel they are part of a single leadership effort, with a shared set of values and way of working.

Using this book

How you use this book is up to you. It's written so you can read it from cover to cover if that's what works for you, or you can just dip into each of the 20 chapters as you need to. We have deliberately structured the book to make it easy to navigate. Each chapter really does do what it 'says on the tin'.

With its deliberate balance of theory and practice, combined with the leadership development tools that are available on our dedicated website, www.honk.org.uk, we hope this book will give you all the tools you need for success. But more than that, we hope we will inspire you in the next stage of your own personal leadership journey, wherever that may take you and with whoever you may lead.

Chapters 2, 3 and 4 of this book provide an opportunity for you to reflect on your personal qualities. What is the moral purpose and motivation that sits behind your approach? Who are you as a leader? How do you tend to respond in certain situations? How well do you know yourself and how able are you to manage your emotions? How do you respond when the going gets tough? These personal characteristics will have a strong influence over your effectiveness every single day. No leader is immune from basic things going wrong. When you have a tough day and one of your client meetings has been a bit of a disaster or you've had a really challenging and unsuccessful meeting with a difficult member of staff, how you manage your emotions and remain positive is highly significant. Your team needs you to remain optimistic in such situations, even when there appears to be absolutely no obvious reason to be so.

Having a strong sense of one's own personal characteristics is a hugely powerful and affirming base from which to lead

For all leaders, having a strong sense of one's own personal characteristics is a hugely powerful and affirming base from which to lead, particularly when the challenges of a leadership role have the potential to become all-consuming.

As a leader, are you clear what your leadership long neck issues are?

Chapters 5 and 6 are all about the importance of context. This is probably the moment to consider what we have named the 'giraffe concept'. At an early age you probably learned that the reason giraffes have evolved to have long necks is so they can reach the leaves on trees that other animals can't. The long neck is the key thing that enables them to be successful and it's the same for all of them. But a quick look at giraffes across the world reveals that, while they may all share similarly long necks, their markings can vary considerably. Some are dark, some lighter. Some have large patches of colour, some smaller. The markings vary according to their environment and the age of the giraffe. They have evolved to suit their context. For us, the same principle applies to the leadership of any organisation. As a leader, are you clear what your leadership *long neck* issues are; the things about leadership you need to know and understand to ensure success? But can you also understand your context and your own predispositions, and can you adapt them to suit your situation, both in terms of what you need to do and how you do it?

Of course, the giraffe concept doesn't just apply to leadership. It is equally relevant when it comes to other facets of business, such as looking at strategies. Different strategies work in different contexts and all organisations and businesses will have a different perspective. So, what's interesting and important is asking *'Under what conditions does this strategy work?'*

Chapters 7 – 18 are the heart of the book. They are all about what you can do to make the biggest difference. Whether you are running a group of companies or have just taken on your first leadership role at a new level, the job is basically the same. Steve Radcliffe, in his brilliantly intuitive *Leadership: plain and simple* (2012), argues that leadership is really only about doing three key things well, which he summarises as Future – Engage – Deliver or 'FED'. The simplicity of his framework is immediately appealing. The more we keep things simple, the better.

> Getting a powerful match between what you are good at and passionate about, and the goals of your team or organisation can make a huge difference to how successful you will be

Future – Engage – Deliver

In the FED model, the first key area focuses on the **future** you envisage for your organisation or team. It relates to your shared vision: what you want your team or organisation to achieve together. Of course, this needs to be backed up with a clear approach to managing those changes in a way that makes the best use of your resources, both financial and human. Ideally, the overall strategy will be based on what you believe will make you most effective, and the degree to which you are keen to try out and evaluate new ideas for yourself. For those in system leadership roles, this is about the strategy underpinning how a group of companies or a group of colleagues can work together successfully. For those of you in your first leadership role, it's about translating wider organisational goals into something tangible and ambitious for your front-line team.

Importantly, Radcliffe argues that to have the greatest success as a leader, you need to care about your vision or goal, and – to use his delightful turn of phrase – you need to be 'up to something'! Getting a powerful match between what you are good at and passionate about, and the goals of your team or organisation can make a huge difference to how successful you will be. Without this, he believes, there's no guarantee of achieving meaningful progress.

Once you are clear on your vision for the future and your strategy for getting there, the next key area of work is to build and sustain great relationships. Only if you **engage** effectively with others can you as a leader at any level make change happen. For CEOs, having a team of management and staff who are committed to shared goals and who work effectively together to achieve them, is at the heart of what makes a great organisation. In other words, this is all about getting collective buy-in to what you want to achieve, and inspiring and enabling others to lead with you. As Radcliffe puts it, whatever leadership role you have, you want to make sure 'the relationships are big enough to get the job done'. Never was that maxim truer than in today's world, where communication is so essential to effectiveness.

The third stage in the model is focused on making sure you **deliver**. Leadership isn't just about strategy and inspiring others, it's about making sure things happen when you want them to, and to the standard you expect. Great organisations are the result of great delivery, and we know that one of the biggest challenges is how to create this consistent delivery for every customer or stakeholder, regardless of their location, their religion, their background or their age.

In any context, great delivery comes from clear systems, processes and support, which enable your people to be great at their jobs, especially your front-line team. It's also about monitoring outcomes and progress to assure consistency and continuous improvement.

No place of work achieves excellence if the leaders responsible for bringing out the best in their management and their people are poorly organised

Primary Colours model

The beauty of Radcliffe's model is its simplicity. But there is another leadership framework, created by David Pendleton (2012) which is very similar to FED and considers, in effect, how each of the three elements interact with one another. For me, with any context in mind, breaking leadership into slightly smaller chunks in this way is useful and resonates with the reality of the job at any level. The figure below shows how the model works.

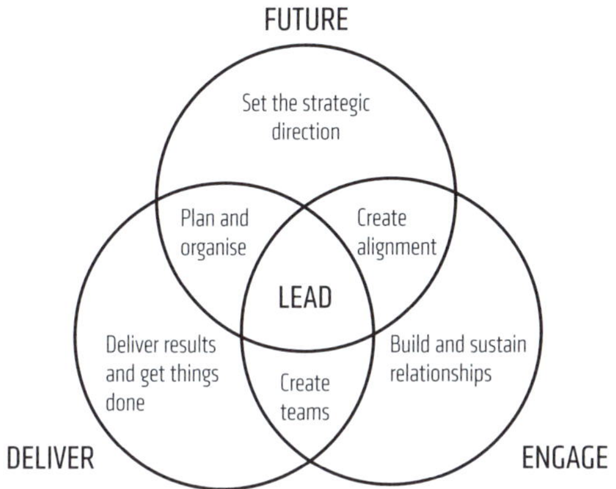

There are some important interplays between the three FED leadership areas. It's no good having a great strategy unless you have **planned** and **organised**. Planning ahead comes more easily to some leaders than others but is critical for us all. No place of work achieves excellence if the leaders responsible for bringing out the best in their management and their people are poorly organised. Apart from the obvious confusion and inefficiency that results, the negative effect on individuals' motivation can be detrimental to their performance.

Your team will be much more effective if everyone is clear as to where you are heading

Secondly, you can lead the most harmonious and motivated team in the world, but if the individuals in it aren't clear on a shared direction of travel, you won't achieve the ambitious goals you are striving for. Creating strong **alignment** is critical and good communication is the lifeblood of an organisation. Whatever level you are leading at, your team will be much more effective if everyone is clear as to where you are heading and has bought into the vision and mission.

Finally, leadership at any level is about leading a team, not doing everything yourself. While it can be very tempting to take on tasks, partly because you know you can usually do the job more quickly and better than others, great leaders **create teams**, delegating tasks and decisions to others. Empowering colleagues in this way, so long as it is done well, has the capacity to significantly increase the quality of delivery overall.

Leadership and management

Distinctions are often made about the difference between leadership and management. Both are critical for the success of a team, a department, a growing company or a group of companies. As the management consultant Peter Drucker said: 'Management is doing things right; leadership is doing the right things.' But sometimes there are times when the distinction between the two can feel artificial. Where, for example, does a good coaching conversation sit? In our view, it is both. You are *leading* by asking great questions which are helping a colleague to develop, and empowering them to lead too. You are *managing* by engaging in a conversation that is usually about improving delivery, performance and, ultimately, customer impact.

This is why David Pendleton's Primary Colours model and Steve Radcliffe's Future-Engage-Deliver model work so well. They both avoid making this distinction while at the same time covering the critical elements of each. Both look at leadership, doing the right things, and the key elements that relate to strategy. Both also give proper attention to delivery and making things happen well. The link between the two is great engagement with those who will make everything work. This book takes the same approach. The focus is on providing models and guidance that leaders at all levels can apply to their context, rather than providing technical descriptions of management techniques such as financial planning and budgeting.

Ultimately, the actions you take as a leader are critical. What you do to create strategy, build relationships and ensure strong delivery will underpin the success of your management team and your people. But it's not quite as simple as that. Your success as a leader isn't just about what you do. It's also about how you lead: your leadership style and how you support and inspire others to develop.

Chapters 19 and 20 discuss the importance for leaders at all levels to be able to adapt their leadership approach to suit their context. In our experience, this usually boils down to properly understanding your people, their performance, and how much time you have. Success in this area can come from developing the critical leadership habit of *asking first*. Using a coaching leadership approach, at least to start with, in a conversation can unlock a much deeper understanding of any situation, enabling adjustments to be made both to what you decide to do and how you decide to do it. Getting your leadership approach right has the potential to significantly enhance the impact of what you do for all those you work with.

Culture and climate

What you do as a leader makes a difference to the results you achieve. But the relationship between leadership and results isn't direct. As shown below, the actions you take as a leader have a significant impact on the culture and climate within your sphere of influence.

LEADERSHIP AND RESULTS
ADAPTED FROM CORPORATE LEADERSHIP COUNCIL (2004)

Culture is essentially 'the way we do things around here'

In this context, *culture* is essentially 'the way we do things around here' and relates to systems, procedures, and common practices delivered to a high standard. A useful way of thinking of culture is to consider what someone new joining your team would see happening on a day-to-day basis and the extent to which everyone in the team is working in the same way and to the same level of expectation. Is there a consistent set of high expectations from you about how your team should work? As a result of this, for example, are the customer service teams you oversee inspiring and well organised? Do employees have strong and supportive relationships with their peers and all the colleagues they work with?

Climate is more about how it *feels* to work in a team. For your team, this reflects its morale, how appreciated your team feels and the degree of trust within the team as a whole. This is much more difficult to describe or measure, but there is evidence to suggest that the effect of climate on team productivity is considerable. This is explored in more detail in the next chapter.

Climate is more about how it feels to work in a team

Discretionary effort

THE MORE POSITIVE THE CULTURE AND CLIMATE YOU CREATE, THE MORE LIKELY YOUR TEAM IS TO GO THE EXTRA MILE

Taken together, the more positive the culture and climate you create, the more likely your team is to go the extra mile. This concept is known as *discretionary effort*. It commonly describes the input from individuals over and above what is required in their contracts. Critical in this context, however, is that this effort is productive. You will probably know of well-meaning and hard-working colleagues who regrettably did not have the impact their efforts deserved because they were too often not sufficiently focused on the right things. In a sales context, it's all very well having fantastically enjoyable meetings and team building sessions but if what the sales team is learning fails to relate to the strategy they are meant to be following or the targets they are striving for, it's all going to be a waste of time.

In other words, it's not about working longer or harder. That can cause stress, burn-out and disaffection which lead to too many people quitting their jobs. It's about caring about one's work in a way that means individuals are constantly striving to improve, to be a tiny bit better tomorrow than they were yesterday.

Getting the culture and climate right can therefore also have an impact on an individual's intention to stay at a place of work, which in turn affects overall retention levels. If you accept the argument that the bigger problem for many organisations is retention not recruitment, then getting these basic conditions right is crucial for everybody involved no matter how big your organisation or business.

Pulling this all together

This figure sums up the overall *Honk!* framework. It forms the basis for the structure of the rest of the book.

THE *HONK!* LEADERSHIP MODEL

Leadership starts with you and your understanding of yourself, the way you tend to behave in certain situations, what you enjoy and are good at, and those areas you should probably focus on if you want to improve your effectiveness. But you also need to take the time to understand your situation properly; the people around you and the context you find yourself in.

Taken together, an understanding of self and situation should enable you to decide what actions you need to prioritise and the best approach to take in implementing them. If you get this right, you will create a productive culture and climate that combine to release significant discretionary effort from those you lead while achieving the outcomes you desire.

Leadership starts with you and your understanding of yourself

You will notice that the first four tiles are shaded. This reflects the fact that they are the key areas where leaders can make changes which will make a difference. The remaining chapters in the book are grouped under these four areas. The outcomes of the changes you make in all these areas will lead to the positive differences in culture, climate and discretionary effort that will bring you the results you want.

Our website, honk.org.uk offers leaders the chance to access high quality online tools to support leadership development. These resources can be used by individuals or groups of leaders alongside this book. Once an organisation has joined the website, it has one year's unlimited access to all the Honk! diagnostic tools listed below for any member of staff in the organisation.

Persona

This online tool asks just 20 questions to create a detailed predisposition report for any leader within an organisation. Based on a Jungian analysis of personality, the tool is designed to help leaders better understand their natural strengths, ways of working and potential areas for growth. Great leadership starts with individuals knowing themselves well, and *Persona* can help all leaders have a greater insight into their leadership predispositions.

360

This tool gives leaders at all levels the chance to rate themselves against 40 key leadership competencies. It also allows leaders to identify colleagues from whom they would like to seek similar feedback. In addition, there is an opportunity for colleagues to give short written feedback on three areas of strength and a potential area for growth. All this feedback is then anonymously collated and automatically emailed back to the leader concerned.

Team

This tool allows members of any team in your organisation to gather views on how effectively that particular team is working. Often used by senior teams, it asks a series of questions that are converted into a visual representation of the team's effectiveness, with suggestions of where the team may want to focus next. It also collects three areas of strength and one potential area for growth from each team member. All this

information is collected anonymously and then automatically mixed up and included in the final report, providing a useful reinforcement of what is working well and some potential areas for growth. The tool is based on the team development model outlined in Chapter 13.

Engage

This tool enables you to measure the degree of discretionary effort or engagement within your team or organisation. By asking ten simple but powerful questions, *Engage* can give you a deeper insight into how much your colleagues care about your team or organisation and are motivated to remain in the organisation and work energetically towards your shared goals. For each question there is an indication of typical response rates, but it is most powerful when used more than once to see how engagement has changed over time.

Unlimited access to all the tools listed above is available for one single membership fee per organisation. To find out more, visit **honk.org.uk**

Nudges

- Do you take time to understand your situation properly before acting?

- How do you make sure you understand your own predispositions fully?

- What is the balance like across the different areas of your leadership actions?

- What do you do to build discretionary effort?

- Change can be challenging; to what extent are you prepared for it?

Travel further together

What everyone in the astronaut corps shares in common is not gender or ethnic background, but motivation, perseverance, and desire – the desire to participate in a voyage of discovery.

ELLEN OCHOA

Ellen Ochoa is an American engineer, former astronaut and the current Director of the John C. Stennis Space Centre in Mississippi. In 1991 she became the first Hispanic female astronaut, flying four missions during her career.

LEADERSHIP AND RESULTS
ADAPTED FROM CORPORATE
LEADERSHIP COUNCIL (2004)

The previous chapter outlined what we mean by discretionary effort and where it fits within the wider *Honk!* model. As the diagram below reminds us, discretionary effort is the product of the culture and climate that our leadership creates.

The Corporate Leadership Council (2004) carried out a survey of organisations of all types from across the world, looking into what builds engagement in employees. As part of this work, it asked thousands of participants how much effect each of the eight key actions that organisations undertake to build discretionary effort had on their levels of motivation. The table below shows what people said.

FACTORS THAT AFFECT ENGAGEMENT
CORPORATE LEADERSHIP COUNCIL (2004)

We think it's interesting to note how bonus pay is such a low motivator, especially given that this survey was carried out in a multitude of businesses as well as in settings such as hospitals, charities and schools. It is also interesting to see how important the induction appears to be. We imagine this is because an individual's first impression of an organisation sticks and can have a profound effect on their expectations and assessment of the culture. Our final reflection is on the importance of the line manager. This is particularly significant for larger organisations, where middle managers – who line manage most of the staff – can elicit discretionary effort more than anyone else right from the beginning.

No wonder middle leadership is often referred to as the engine room of larger organisations

What is it that leaders of all organisations can do that will have the biggest impact on discretionary effort? Each of the tiles in the diagram below contains ideas that we believe build engagement. Some elements, like *clarity*, are not that exciting, but are fundamental when it comes to creating buy-in. If people don't know what is expected of them, the required culture will not develop and discretionary effort will inevitably dissipate. Others, like *openness, transparency and trust* are more about creating the conditions that enable people to feel more positive about their workplace and their role within it.

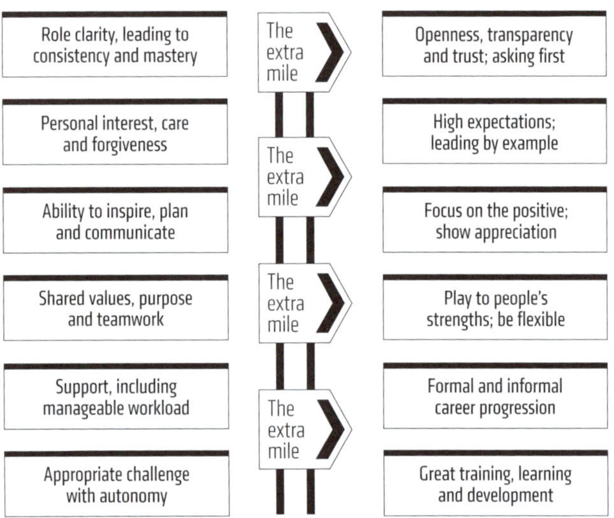

BUILDING DISCRETIONARY EFFORT

Try to avoid falling into the trap of believing these are all about the warm and fluffy stuff. A great culture includes high expectations combined with appropriate challenge and support.

> **If people don't know what is expected of them, the required culture will not develop**

FEELING MOTIVATED TO WORK MORE EFFECTIVELY

As mentioned in Chapter 1, greater engagement or discretionary effort doesn't, indeed *shouldn't*, mean that people are working longer and longer hours. It is about people feeling motivated to work more effectively. In fact, if your staff are working longer and longer hours and looking more and more exhausted, this should act as a flag to you that your systems may need a tweak or two. Mary Portas, better known as Mary Queen of Shops, states: 'This simply isn't the modern way; gruelling working practices are becoming less and less acceptable with younger employees, and rightly so.' Mary puts her money where her mouth is and positively encourages her colleagues to make time for a balanced life. And yes, she not only talks the talk but walks the walk, working from home as often as she can. 'Businesses have to be kinder,' she says, 'There's a whole generation saying: "Hang on, I don't want to work that way". Millennials are unwilling to accept punishing hours. Companies need to adapt and recognise the wants and needs of a new generation if they are to be successful. Tomorrow's businesses will be built on collaboration and understanding, and people will bring their whole selves to work and not aim for profit at all costs.'

MARY PORTAS

What motivates us?

In his book *Drive*, Daniel Pink (2011) gives us a very simple and powerful synthesis of what motivates us at work. Based on extensive and respected psychological research, he identifies:

DANIEL PINK

1. Purpose – caring about what we are doing and why it matters.

2. Mastery – the opportunity for us to get really good at something.

3. Autonomy – having the freedom to innovate and personalise what we do.

All three of his key areas feature in the model above and all three are eminently possible to achieve in the workplace. But sometimes leaders can take the first for granted, or they might put the second at risk by changing too much too quickly, or reduce the benefits from the third by overly specifying in minute detail how people should be doing their jobs. The best leaders are either consciously or intuitively tuned into their teams and their context to make sure they get this balance right.

The best leaders are either consciously
or intuitively tuned into their teams

As well as building discretionary effort, a productive culture and climate have a positive effect on staff retention, which is a basic building block for creating consistency.

RICHARD BRANSON

As Richard Branson says: 'Train people well enough so they can leave; treat them well enough so that they don't want to'. Given the challenges that never seem to go away when it comes to recruitment in many areas, reducing the requirement to attract new managers and staff by retaining those you already have, makes a great deal of sense.

Train people well enough so they can leave; treat them well enough so that they don't want to

THE STARS IN YOUR ORGANISATION

We're sure you can all think of those absolute gems in your organisation, the people we later refer to as your 'stars' in Chapter 6. Pay close attention to how you treat them and see the difference it makes to your work place. Yes, of course some people will come and go, but if you build your culture and create bonds you'll be stronger and will deal with that in a better way, from a more stable position.

The zone of growth

The last model we would like to share in this chapter originates from the work of psychologists Yerkes and Dodson (1908). It suggests there is a powerful link between how challenging tasks are to complete, and the impact they have on our development. If we stay in our comfort zone, doing things we find easy most of the time, unsurprisingly our personal development is steady but limited. When we are in the zone of stretch or growth, the impact on our learning and development is suddenly much higher.

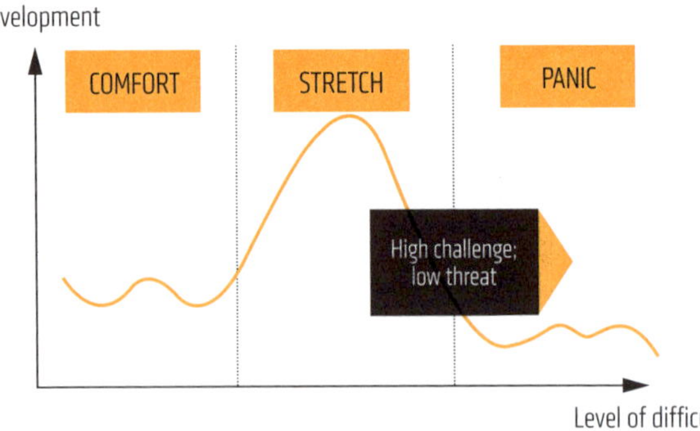

THE ZONE OF STRETCH
ADAPTED FROM YERKES AND DODSON (1908)

Typically, the model suggests the zone of growth is 10-15% outside one's zone of comfort. The concept is powerful and can be applied to everyone. If you can create a situation where your staff are in the zone of stretch for large parts of their day, step back and watch what happens. By being more motivated to be a little better tomorrow than they were yesterday, your team or organisation will just keep getting better.

There is however, a limit to how far we can push into the zone of stretch. If the level of difficulty is too high – and we would argue this can be in terms of cognitive challenge or through the sheer volume of work that is expected – then personal welfare and self-belief start to become an issue and individuals will find themselves in the zone of panic or stress. If people are in this zone for long periods of time, there is a risk of well-being or mental health issues developing.

Having read Mary Myatt's inspiring book, *High Challenge, Low Threat* (2016) we are reminded of our ability as both leaders and senior managers to metaphorically move the line separating growth and panic. If we can create an environment of mutual trust and respect, where it is OK to try difficult things even if we make mistakes, then we can enable our teams and our colleagues to take on more challenging tasks without getting to those stress or panic points.

Nudges

- How would you characterise the culture and climate in your team or organisation?

- What could you do to build discretionary effort in your context?

- How are you doing with regard to staff retention?

- To what extent do you enable your team to develop and grow? Would Daniel Pink's 1, 2 ,3 help?

- How useful is the concept of the zones of comfort, growth and panic?

- How do you help colleagues to keep stretching themselves?

Be wonderful to work with

Leaders come in many forms, with many styles and diverse qualities. There are quiet leaders and leaders one can hear in the next county. Some find strength in eloquence, some in judgment, some in courage.

JOHN W. GARDNER

John W. Gardner was born in 1912, he had a varied and productive career as an educator, public official, and political reformer. Perhaps best known as the founder of the people's lobby Common Cause, he was the author of several best-selling books on the themes of achieving personal and societal excellence.

What's it like to work with you? A useful starting point is how well you know yourself and can manage your emotions. This can have a big impact on how well you are able to build relationships with others and help to bring out the best in them.

Andy leads here with his thoughts:

For as long as I can remember, I have read about the importance of leaders knowing themselves. I have to admit that it was only toward the end of my second school headship, after more than 15 years in senior leadership roles, that I began to take this principle seriously. It sounded like the sort of thing someone who wasn't in a leadership position might say: something of theoretical interest but of little practical relevance.

As the leader of a school, what mattered to me was working out the right thing to do and getting everyone doing it to a high standard. I understood the need to assess a situation, and I appreciated the importance of developing strategy. I knew it mattered to get others on board and excited about what we wanted to achieve. I knew it was important to monitor progress and outcomes closely to see how we were doing.

But what I didn't allow for were my own predispositions in all of that. All of us respond to situations in different ways, both emotionally and rationally.

We bring all sorts of preconceptions and predispositions to situations. We are, to a greater or lesser extent, able to read the emotions of others accurately and manage our own in as much as we can recognise them. All of this, of course, has an impact on making good decisions or forming effective relationships.

I can recall many situations when, for whatever reason, things didn't always work out the way I had hoped. When I look back on my first school headship, my default reaction was usually to blame, not to try to find out why something hadn't worked. This was often followed by trying, usually single-handedly, to find a solution and then pretty much impose it on everyone else. Alongside this, I was quick to make judgements about others' competence, and sometimes people decided it was best to leave the school. Of course, in many cases this was the right thing. Great schools, to use Jim Collins' analogy in Good to Great (2001), are good at getting the right people on the bus and the wrong people off. As a leader at any level, we need to be clear about the standards we expect and hold others to account, but I think I was too quick to act in some of those situations. I am naturally predisposed to take swift and decisive action without always taking the time to think something through. It is a preference I am still working to manage; a habit I am still modifying.

JIM COLLINS

Sharing your predispositions with others can also be powerful. If colleagues know the things you are good at and enjoy doing, the whole team can benefit from those strengths. If there are things that energise you, let others know. Conversely, if there are particular behaviours that de-motivate or irritate you, let others know these too. Finally, if there are predispositions you are working to manage more effectively, it can be helpful to tell colleagues. Not only can they give you feedback when you are doing well on these, which is helpful, they can also give a gentle reminder when you are not.

Emotional intelligence

The turn of the century saw the emergence of the concept of emotional intelligence (EQ). Setting aside the debate about whether this is an intelligence at all, or simply a set of personal competences, in his seminal article for the Harvard Business Review, *Leadership that gets results* (2000), Daniel Goleman's model brought the idea to international prominence. He suggests that a leader's EQ is likely to be a much more important indicator of their effectiveness than their cognitive intelligence (IQ). Of course, IQ is important, but Goleman argues that the thing which distinguishes standout performance is much more likely to be EQ. This makes a lot of sense to us because in both the private and public sectors we need to deliver through others if we are to deliver great outcomes for

A LEADER'S EQ IS LIKELY TO BE A MUCH MORE IMPORTANT INDICATOR OF THEIR EFFECTIVENESS THAN THEIR COGNITIVE INTELLIGENCE (IQ)

DANIEL GOLEMAN

MIKE BREARLEY

customers or stakeholders. Mike Brearley in his book, *The Art of Captaincy*, (2001) described the similarity between a team captain and an NHS manager and said: 'Both must absorb and understand the anxieties of colleagues and team members.' Brearley concluded: 'There is no substitute for the leader's capacity to bring people together in a common task, so that people come to take pleasure in their joint and individual work.' We can't do everything ourselves, so building great relationships is critical. The strength of Goleman's model is its simplicity. He identified four key domains for emotional intelligence, which are set out below.

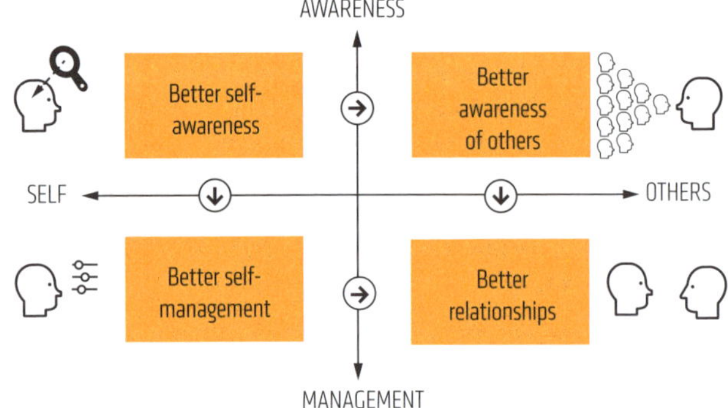

A MODEL OF EMOTIONAL INTELLIGENCE
DANIEL GOLEMAN

As the model summarises, Goleman believes emotional intelligence begins with increased self-awareness. This in turn supports one's awareness of others and provides an opportunity for you to manage your own emotions. Together, the combination of these two provide the basis by which one can build better relationships. The level of self-awareness in leaders pretty much defines their ability to build relationships with others, which is critical to their effectiveness.

Being able to identify situations that arouse strong emotions means you can identify and interpret those emotions and then manage the situation more effectively

Understanding your emotional responses

While colleagues or senior managers can see how you behave in a difficult conversation, none will usually be able to identify how you are feeling inside. A difficult discussion with a member of your team who might require disciplinary action because they have gone off the rails and allowed personal issues to interfere with their work will arouse a range of emotions. And how are you likely to feel if you realise you have to make significant budget cuts and make colleagues redundant?

These feelings are natural and in no way a sign of failure. If you can notice them and observe what kinds of situations trigger stress or emotional responses in you, then you have a better chance of remaining in control of a situation. Being able to identify situations that arouse strong emotions means you can identify and interpret those emotions and then manage the situation more effectively. It also allows you to sustain a valid perspective. A powerful strategy can be to reflect on a situation by imagining yourself stepping outside your body and viewing your situation from a different perspective. What would that tell you?

How about looking at sport, to give a different perspective on this issue? Rob has been managing Chichester Hockey Men's 1st Team for the past two seasons and spent his second season working closely with new Dutch coach Merijn Van Willigen. Prior to Merijn's arrival, he was too open with his emotions during a match, feeling that the team were driven by his passion. He would fire off at umpires and the opposition managers alike. On arrival Merijn quickly pointed out: 'We don't want to be that team, we will keep calm, we will keep the team calm, keep our bench calm and this will help us concentrate our focus.' Rob freely admits that Merijn taught him to be cooler and to allow for periods of calm. He now approaches matches, and most importantly, umpires very differently. Together the coaching team remain calmer on the touchline, which allows them to think clearly as a group, especially during those powder-keg moments on the pitch that are so typical in sport.

MERIJN VAN WILLIGEN

It begs the question; what type of touchline manager would you be?

WHAT TYPE OF TOUCHLINE MANAGER WOULD YOU BE?

Role-modelling self-awareness

Ideally, you want to build a culture and climate in your own team where self-awareness is valued and practised. It can be powerful for your team to see their role model being self-aware or acting as a 'learning-centred leader'. One of the most striking ways to do this is for you to admit that you do not know the answer to something, or that you need the support of your team to solve a problem. Continuous learning and reflection is to be celebrated and is an important part of developing as a leader. Andy notes the importance of having your own role models and it may be worth telling your team about them.

PATRICK LENCIONI

If you are feeling confident, you might even admit a development area or a challenge and invite feedback or ideas from colleagues. In *The Advantage*, Patrick Lencioni (2014) describes a range of team exercises that use the sharing of feedback as a mechanism for building trust and establishing a culture of reflection. For example, you might invite your team to give you feedback on how you could have handled a situation differently. By putting yourself in the position of receiving feedback, you powerfully model the value of reflection and self-awareness. At the same time, this process is not a finger pointing exercise. It needs to be focused and deliberate, initiated by you, conducted by you and concluded by thanking everybody for their input.

> By putting yourself in the position of receiving feedback, you powerfully model the value of reflection and self-awareness

Your own EQ profile

So what are the key components of emotional intelligence in Goleman's model?

Better self-awareness

- Ask others about your strengths and weaknesses, using 360 feedback, if useful and appropriate.

- Become more finely attuned to the physical reactions you have in certain situations and learn to recognise them.

- Keep a diary of your emotional shifts.

- Notice how you react in each case. What do you think? Are there any physical responses? What would others see you do?

- If you notice an emotional reaction in yourself, try to identify the cause.

- Know your emotional triggers. You can then respond in a purposeful, controlled way, rather than automatically.

Better awareness of others

- Remember that when it comes to expressing emotions, most of what you communicate comes from your tone of voice and body language rather than the actual words you use.

- Watch for mirroring of body language in others.

- Watch TV programmes or films with the sound turned down and see what you observe.

- Watch live sports on TV and study the managers and how they behave.

- Ask more open questions. Be neutral in the way you ask them, so people say what they really think.

- Listen more closely for deep understanding.

- Look for the way people behave in meetings, not just what they say.

- Look for what's *not* being said.

- Avoid finishing others' sentences.

- Check for understanding.

Better self-management

- This is not about controlling emotions but managing your responses most productively.

- Take responsibility for your emotions. You create them, not others.

- Do something that requires you to think rationally.

- Have letters or emails about your successes that you can read when you feel like you have lost your confidence.

- Learn to reflect in the moment. Use this thinking time to detach yourself from the emotion.

Better relationships

- Affirm throughout a conversation, especially when not talking.

- Paraphrase and summarise. Show you have listened.

- Under promise and over deliver.

- Find out what matters to other people. Are they, for example, motivated by moral purpose, or the logic of an argument, or your passion or just by gaining power and influence?

- Be gently proactive in maintaining communication. Don't wait for them.

- Praise in writing.

- Challenge face-to-face.
- Talk less than you listen.

'Know thyself' was written on the forecourt of the Temple of Apollo at Delphi as a message to the philosophers, statesmen and law-givers who laid the foundation for western culture. It is one of the greatest challenges for every leader: to know their strengths and development areas, to know what arouses strong emotions in themselves and how to manage these.

If you are a middle manager, stepping into a leadership role for the first time, your voyage of self-discovery is usually faster than it will be at any other point in your career. You are learning all the time, taking on new responsibilities, managing up and down, and often still have a pretty full schedule and little time to step back and reflect.

For senior managers too, the journey to self-awareness never ends

Your experiences and strengths in your previous role have helped you reach your middle management position, and while you need to retain those strengths in your new role, you are now exposing yourself to new challenges which will create new development areas. This is where senior managers can really add value. They can help you identify your new development areas and support you, through mentoring and coaching, to build your skills in these areas. They can also help you reflect on how you are progressing.

But for senior managers too, the journey to self-awareness never ends. As we've mentioned earlier, it took rather too long for some of us at *Honk!* to realise the potential and power of strong self-awareness in our own lives!

And remember the Dalai Lama once said: 'We must lead a way of life with self-awareness and compassion, to do as much as we can. Then whatever happens we will have no regrets.'

Knowing yourself

There are several ways you can get to know yourself better. You can try to face your demons and be honest with yourself by trying to recognise your real strengths and weaknesses; we all have them and we all need help in different areas. Another way, of course, is to build honest and open relationships so people just say it to you as it is. But this isn't always easy to do, particularly when it comes to getting feedback from people within your team. One way round this is for you to take part in a more structured 360 feedback survey. There are a few variations on how a 360 survey can be conducted, but they are generally designed to allow you to reflect on your own strengths and areas for development and then see how this aligns with the perceptions of about five other colleagues. This feedback will usually come from a range of individuals: those who are more senior than you, your peers and those who are part of your team. In other words, they represent a 360 degree view.

While these are starting to become a little more commonplace than they were a few years ago, we are a long way from all management viewing 360 survey tools as a routine part of the feedback they should expect to receive to support their development. Part of the reason for this is that it has either been too expensive or too time consuming to operate 360 surveys for all leaders in a business, as sometimes it's hard to see the value. However, there are plenty of online options that businesses can consider, some of which represent excellent value. At *Honk!* we have created our own anonymous and fully automated 360 survey tool, with 40 questions structured around the leadership model underpinning this book, as well as the opportunity to offer other feedback on personal strengths and potential areas for growth.

You might also consider using one of the many online personality tools available to increase self-awareness. A popular example is the Myers-Briggs Type Indicator (MBTI) which gives an indication of behavioural preferences in four opposing areas. At *Honk!* we have developed an online tool that is also based on a Jungian model of personality type, called *Persona*. As with any of these personality tools, don't use the outcome of any process to help you justify to yourself or others why you can or can't do certain things. For example, someone who likes leaving things to the last minute and prefers to keep things open and flexible (which can be a strength in certain situations) shouldn't allow this to be a reason why they can't be better organised. Just like writing with your other hand, it is just a bit more difficult and takes more deliberate practice.

It's also worth reflecting on the best way to use any personality tool. For us, we must accept that all tools will have their limitations. Take MBTI, for example. It is one of the most commonly used personality instruments right across the globe, yet there are those who challenge whether there is enough evidence to support the efficacy of the instrument itself. We suspect arguments about this and other tools will always be with us, so it seems to us that a sensible and pragmatic

PERSONA

approach to using any tool might be to follow these steps: (i) take part in the review process, (ii) look at what emerges and then (iii) decide for oneself what is helpful and just focus on that. In other words, just use a personality tool to help shed a little light on oneself and then take it from there, rather than becoming fixated on one's personality type. This approach allows you to focus on what really matters: using such tools to support self-reflection and personal development.

Using 360 feedback

Using personality predisposition tools and 360 feedback will allow you to reflect on your own strengths and areas for growth, as well as compare your own perceptions with those of your colleagues. This may confirm what you knew already or, more helpfully, tell you something you didn't know. The Johari window (Luft and Ingham, 1955) is a model that groups these areas into four categories:

1. *Open*, which are those known by you and others.

2. *Hidden*, which are known by you but which you do not reveal to others.

3. *Blind spot*, which are those others know about you, but you do not know about yourself.

4. *Unknown* which are those that are not known to you or others.

The unknown areas are the hardest to discover and, apart from using 360 feedback, often the best way to find them is when you put yourself in new or particularly challenging situations, when more concealed emotions are often heightened and become more evident.

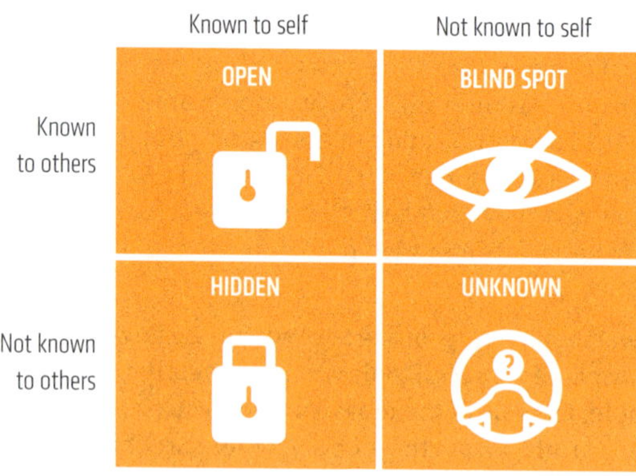

Consistent review

Whatever your leadership role, making time to review your own performance regularly is a useful habit to develop.

There are four ways you can do this:

- Make time to reflect – do you systematically and regularly make time to think about the effectiveness of your leadership practice?

- Ask for feedback – do you make a point of asking for feedback from colleagues, team members and your managers?

- Practise mindfulness – what strategies do you use to relax and create the mental space for you to reflect?

- Critical friend – who do you speak to beyond your line manager to process your thoughts and ideas and get an external perspective on your challenges? Might you benefit from having a coach, particularly if you are facing an exciting but slightly daunting leadership transition?

The power of humility

When Jim Collins in his book *Good to Great* (2001) looked at the companies which his methodology judged had made the move from good to great, he discovered something very interesting about the leaders of those companies. Unsurprisingly, all of them were very ambitious. However, this ambition was not focused on their own achievements but on being ambitious for their organisation. They were, in fact, very modest about their own personal achievements. When they talked about their companies, it was more as if their successes were a result of a huge team effort of which they had the privilege to be at the helm. The key for these leaders of course is for their team to follow the same ethos to support the culture and not allow individual egos to get in the way of the success of the company. As C.S. Lewis reminds us, 'Humility is not thinking less of yourself; it's thinking of yourself less'.

When Andy was responsible for running the London Challenge *Good to Great* programme, as the head of a school that was judged 'good' at the time, he used to invite heads from schools that had been judged 'outstanding' three or four times, to come to conferences and talk about their journeys. When listening to these successful school leaders, exactly the same phenomenon that Jim Collins identified emerged strongly. The heads all extolled the virtues of their staff, pupils and the support they received from the families in their communities. Of course, they acknowledged the importance of their own personal leadership and their drive for continuous improvement, but they were all modest about their achievements, wanting always to give the credit to others rather than to themselves.

> But the definition of humility here is not about false modesty; these leaders have a grounded and honest sense of who has achieved what

In some ways, this finding isn't too surprising. After all, this is exactly the type of leadership that will build trust among staff and team members and help people to develop themselves while learning in the workplace. It will also encourage an open, honest and transparent environment where leaders have the emotional intelligence and self-awareness to recognise the importance of celebrating the achievements of everyone, while at the same time keeping the focus on performance and continuous improvement. And don't forget the team will also be watching and learning these skills from their mentor.

But the definition of humility here is not about false modesty; these leaders have a grounded and honest sense of who has achieved what. They are confident about their own abilities and don't need to prove themselves to others by advertising their own achievements.

Respecting uncertainty

MICHAEL FULLAN

But as Michael Fullan points out in *The six secrets of change* (2008) there is another reason that effective leaders remain humble. He was writing about schools, which are no different from any other organisation in that they operate within an incredibly complex environment, and any leader who is not humbled by the complexities of such a complicated context and who doesn't recognise the need to keep learning and keep up to speed with the developments around them is unlikely to remain as a leader in a high performing organisation. For example, issues such as how we should use new technologies like social networking to support learning, what we now know about how the brain works, the challenges of recruiting staff and the rapid changes to population demographics all present school leaders with an ever-changing landscape. The same issues of a shifting environment and a constantly evolving market place can apply to organisations in any sector and therefore it makes sense to try and learn from each other. The same issues will rise again and again and will only vary in their application to the context.

Building momentum, loyalty and trust

There is also clear evidence that leaders who don't see themselves as being above certain types of work have a strong impact on building momentum. All leaders, however senior, can reap the benefits of being 'hands on'. Leaders who are prepared to demonstrate that they have both the ability and willingness to tackle the tasks they expect everyone else to do, not only gain huge personal respect, but they help create the kind of alignment that builds organisational momentum.

Demonstrating this willingness to carry out any role also builds trust, particularly when taking the time to join with others in what might be seen as more menial tasks such as reorganising the office space, helping a colleague with a technical issue or taking your turn to make the coffee for your team. Try to carry out the act naturally and not for reward and watch the loyalty which that simple act buys, loyalty which will inevitably be multiplied ten times over. You may already take this kind of action, but if you don't, consider the culture you could create with just a small shift in behaviour.

In 2011, the All Blacks beat France in a World Cup pool game at their home ground at Eden Park in Auckland. Richie McCaw, who they say has titanium running through his veins and who has captained the All Blacks in 110 of his 148 test matches received his 100th cap. At the presentation he spoke of needing time to understand his achievements

RICHIE MCCAW

and most importantly he thanked his mum. Four years later in the following World Cup Ma'a Nonu who was one of the 'team leaders' played his 100th match for the All Blacks and was presented with his cap by his long term captain and friend Richie. Ma'a gave an emotional acceptance speech thanking the Lord, his family and his team saying 'I love you brothers' in what was another successful night for him and this juggernaut of a team.

After the match the press gathered to meet the brothers in arms only to be told that the two centurions would be a little late as they were cleaning the changing rooms. When the surprised press corps showed their annoyance at being kept waiting, they were reminded that the All Blacks team always leave the dressing rooms cleaner than they found them and that every squad member takes their turn with this work. On this occasion it was the turn of Richie and Ma'a to do the clean-up.

A captain or leader is no better than anyone else. Such acts show a deep-rooted understanding that the leaders involved are part of a team, where everyone is essential and where these small acts build respect for their surroundings and for every person in the group.

A focus on the business, the organisation or the team, not the leader

In drawing this chapter to a close, remember that we are certainly not saying the best leaders lack ambition, competitiveness or drive. They are focused on achieving the best they can for their organisation, their group or team. What sets the leaders in the best organisations apart is that their ambition is for the business, organisation or team itself, not for themselves as an individual.

The most successful leaders want the best for their team

This links back to the importance of moral purpose, where the most successful leaders want the best for their team. Of course, it is important that their work is enjoyable, fun and personally rewarding, but we can't stress enough that the main motivator is the success of the organisation, not their own progression as an individual leader. All Blacks legend Richie McCaw said: 'The first day I put on the jersey I just didn't want to let it down, I wanted to add to a 100-year legacy.'

Nudges

- Have you considered your strengths and potential areas for growth in relation to EQ?

- Where might you want to focus on building your EQ competence and what are you going to do?

- Do you know your own predispositions as a leader?

- Do you play to your strengths?

- Are there any areas you know you need to keep in mind and try to manage more effectively as they have the potential to limit your effectiveness?

- How can others help you achieve this?

- Do you give credit to others for the success of your team, organisation or business?

- Are you prepared to lead by example in any role and not portray yourself as being too important to do certain types of work?

Bounce back when the going gets tough

> *Success is not final, failure is not fatal.
> It is the courage to continue that counts.*

WINSTON CHURCHILL

British Prime Minister from 1940-45 and 1951-1955. He is best
remembered for successfully leading Britain through World War 2 and
was famous for his inspiring speeches and for his refusal to give in,
even when things were going badly.

If you have courage to do the right thing, trust your judgement and keep going even when the going gets tough, there is no limit to what you can achieve.

The challenges for new leaders

The first rung of leadership can be tough. You suddenly find yourself responsible for other people and what they do. They make demands of you. You want to bring out the best in them, but can lack the confidence to really challenge your team, especially if some of them are more experienced or older than you. And at the same time, there are people above you making demands too. What is sometimes called middle leadership can feel like being caught between the devil and the deep blue sea. Yet front-line leadership is often where the real difference can be made. As we saw in Chapter 2, line-managers can make the biggest difference when it comes to building discretionary effort.

You must be disciplined with your day, know what's important and is a priority, and what's not so important, so as to give yourself enough time to master your role. Technology has removed physical barriers, so you can be reached anywhere at any time, which can be exhausting and limit your time to escape and think. Manage those around you, and make sure you know when to say 'no' and dare we say it, out of hours, know when to switch your phone off.

SIMONE FRANGHI

Simone Franghi, once chairman of Tie Rack, which in the 90s had 450 stores said: *'If you cannot do your job in eight hours, then you are not doing your work properly.'* According to Professor Sir Cary Cooper, the famous organisation psychologist, any more than that is likely to make you ill over time.

SIR CARY COOPER

Senior leadership

We guess it's obvious that as a manager, while the potential impact of your work and the decisions you make can be much greater in a more senior role, so too can the potential for pressure and anxiety increase. Decisions you take have bigger implications for you personally, the organisation, your team and, most importantly, your customers or stakeholders if things go wrong. The pressure of accountability, particularly for CEOs, directors and senior managers is significant. These pressures are sometimes self-imposed, and sometimes not, and can occur when the organisation is performing effectively just as easily as when it's struggling. When things are going well, expectations can escalate, and your results can be harder to achieve. Great team members come and go and change your team dynamics forcing you to be adaptable. Understanding that the world, and your environment, will keep changing will help you to be grounded in reality when those challenges inevitably come.

KNOW WHEN TO SWITCH YOUR PHONE OFF

Understanding that the world, and your environment, will keep changing will help you to be grounded in reality when those challenges inevitably come

The pressure that comes from dealing with unforeseen circumstances will really test your resolve, and you can pretty much guarantee that these problems never come at an optimal time. In the case of employees, you can get caught up in the emotional connection as well; maybe a colleague gets ill or, worse still, dies and you are left to soldier on. In such circumstances the best leaders seem to be able to draw on a source of inspiration deep inside themselves and lead their team through a tough time.

So, what is it that great leaders at all levels do which makes a difference?

In order to stay strong for your team, you have to stay strong yourself

Managing your emotions

In order to stay strong for your team, you have to stay strong yourself, which means managing your emotions, as we saw in Chapter 3. Learn how different situations make you feel stressed and keep in mind that emotions are not a sign of weakness. In fact, recognising and identifying how you are feeling is a real strength; remember it's the 21st century and you are allowed to express your feelings. The important thing is to acknowledge your emotions but not be governed by them, and if you can recognise your emotions, then you probably know how to manage them. Maybe when you feel stressed or worried you need to talk to someone you trust to get a different perspective. Maybe you need to create some personal space to think through the problem. Maybe you need to go for a run or do something different to clear your head. But leave the Malbec alone, for now.

Some questions to ask yourself might include:

- How do I feel?
- Why do I feel that way (for example a recent event, or criticism)?
- What assumptions am I making?
- Are those assumptions totally valid?
- What would I tell myself to do if I were observing from outside?
- Who can I talk to and trust in times of need?

The game is only over when you give up

Turning negativity into positivity

In the moments of highest pressure and negative criticism, you have two choices: you can either allow the criticism to grow and descend into a negative spiral, dragging you down into a terrible state. Or, you can try to analyse your response to whatever has triggered your feelings and deal with them positively. Try and get someone you trust to help you think things through. Strong leaders are quick to admit when they get something wrong, and demonstrating that you are listening will help prove to others that you want to adapt, improve, learn and grow with them. Show that you can turn negative situations into positive ones. The game is only over when you give up.

It is useful to put yourself in the position of the person giving feedback or criticism. Often they may just want to voice frustration; they may be under pressure themselves which they are projecting onto you, or they may really care and only sound negative because they want things to be better. Try and see each occasion as an opportunity to learn about your team and yourself. Rob's father's mantra as a flying instructor in the early 70s was: 'From our pupils we learn.'

Fergal was newly appointed to a position on the management team of a school in Kent and announced rather formally that he'd be observing people's lessons, which threw them into a state of defensiveness. He quickly realised how abrupt he had been and wrote a message to all the staff apologising for his insensitivity. Rather than worrying as to how much loss of face he had suffered, he realised that people were grateful for an admission of having got things wrong. Fergal ended up gaining rather than losing people's support.

You can't lose if you respond positively, work hard to avoid taking things personally and always, always behave professionally. Tap into why your colleagues are behaving the way they are and then you can use their feedback to build support. Try to avoid meeting fire with fire, however tempting this may be. Be aware of your body language, your tone of voice and most importantly, show your ability to listen.

You may weigh everything up and decide you were right and, if that's the case, it's a win-win because you dealt with your team in a positive way and used the feedback to build support.

Once you have made up your mind as to what you are going to do in a situation, make your team aware of your decision, and make sure everybody commits to the changes you want to make. Remember that they have all been part of this process, but now it's time to lead. Show your commitment and motivation and be positive that the team can succeed going forward.

Some questions you may want to ask:

- How are they behaving (anger, frustration, or commitment)?

- What are they saying (do they want improvement, change, or vindication)?

- What is behind the words (influence, affirmation, or veiled support)?

- What do they want to hear (apology, commitment to change, or that they are right)?

Staying optimistic

Jon Coles, CEO of United Learning and a former director general at the Department for Education, suggests that leaders need to exhibit *unwarranted optimism*. Team members look to leaders when things are difficult. They need to see leaders being positive about the future, however hard this is to achieve, to make them feel secure in difficult or uncertain circumstances. There is no doubt that positivity will breed positivity in your team or department.

Leaders need to exhibit unwarranted optimism

Here are some practical ways this can be achieved:

- Recognising and celebrating small successes to build momentum and positivity in the team.

- Praising the team to keep them positive; you will find this makes you more positive too.

- Communicating so that others hear your voice regularly and you control the flow of information and messages.

- Being authentic and honest so people feel they can trust you to deliver a tough message when it is required.

- Copying role models – when you are feeling vulnerable, copy the behaviour of others who appear in control.

- Communicating your vision – this will inspire the team and remind them about the big picture and the reasons behind what you are doing.

- Communicating your mission – keep your organisation's mission statement clearly visible and make sure your team understand and follow it.

Learning and improving from criticism

Criticism is by nature a negative behaviour but used wisely can help you learn and develop. It's important in the first place not to analyse it in the moment. Often it is hard to be objective about criticism under pressure when you are receiving it because emotions, sensitivities and fears are heightened. There seems to be a default reaction to criticism, where people immediately try to deflect fault and look to blame others. Remember, you are not actually being physically threatened, so your evolved reaction, fight or flight, is not appropriate. Listen to what's being said, then you'll be half way to turning a negative into a positive. The most effective organisations and people are keen to learn from their mistakes. However painful, it's the most effective way of learning. Learn from your mistakes and try to avoid repeating the same behaviour. We know it hurts, but show gratitude to people for pointing out how you can improve. We know!

> **The most effective organisations and people are keen to learn from their mistakes**

A useful exercise is to keep a log of feedback, problems and your actions, so you can reflect once the crisis has passed and everybody has found something to be positive about. You then have a safe space to review and analyse what has happened. It would also be good to practise letting everyone share their perspectives and what they would do in your situation. Make sure that face to face conversations are held in private and not in public, especially if you need to have tough conversations.

Keeping going

Some people do not retire. Ranulph Fiennes, described as 'the world's greatest living explorer' by the *Guinness Book of Records*, is one of them. In 2000 he amputated two of his fingers using a fretsaw and a vice after his wife said he had become 'irritable' from frostbite pain, and even in his 70s he is still running marathons across continents, so it's not like he's not bothered by problems of old age.

We often draw strength and learning from people outside of business because we are all on a journey and to overcome any challenge we

need to follow similar principles. Nothing happens overnight, it's the culmination of hard work over a significant period of time which builds the momentum needed to get the job done. Be prepared to have determination and self-belief and remember you will always have to be seen to be leading. Don't be surprised if just when you think you have everything sorted, something else crops up, but as you grow in strength, your belief will grow, and dealing with issues should become easier. As Ranulph Fiennes said: 'There is of course never any point in crying over spilt milk, the key is to learn from failures and then keep going.'

There is of course never any point in crying over spilt milk, the key is to learn from failures and then keep going

Taking calculated risks

All leaders, senior managers and middle managers need to take risks, and doing so demands courage in itself. Our entrepreneurial brains, which can be impulsive, tell us that taking risks is essential to achieve anything in life, but our survivor instincts drive us to manage risk. Indeed, managing risk has to be a core focus that as CEOs, leaders and managers we continuously improve. Understanding that risk comes in many shapes and sizes and levels of degree is useful, for instance if you are going to give relatively junior members of staff key roles or tasks within your team, you are creating a risk that can easily backfire. Stretching junior team members is admirable and can help to create a culture where people learn on the job and develop themselves, but you need to manage that risk carefully. In Australia, where Rob has lived and worked, there is an expectation that an individual will be responsible for their actions from a young age and risk management is part of life.

Stretching junior team members is admirable and can help to create a culture where people learn on the job and develop themselves, but you need to manage that risk carefully

In the UK however, we have gradually removed as much risk as possible from children's lives rather than teaching them to manage it, meaning that in the eyes of many commentators we have created a 'snowflake' generation which lacks resilience. Fergal was determined to keep the spirit of adventure that existed in the school he led by continuing to allow relatively young children to venture into the woods adjacent to the school. To mitigate the risk of anyone getting hurt, it was a clearly understood rule that children could only enter the woods in groups of at least three. All children knew the point of this: if someone got hurt, one person stayed with them, while the other could go and get help. Yes there was risk, but it was mitigated.

On the other hand, we're sure you can all think of examples when you've been cautious and it's paid off. It's having a method to calculate your decisions, often under pressure, which is a key skill to develop.

A model of school leadership in challenging urban environments (National College of School Leadership, 2004) describes how the best leaders show courage by:

- standing up for their beliefs and defending them in the face of opposition and entrenched interests

- doing the right thing rather than taking the easy option, despite the possible risks and complications

- taking calculated risks, where appropriate.

When you consider the importance of decision making and risk calculation that school leaders need to take, you will appreciate that as business leaders we can learn from some of their methods.

A model for resilience

One useful model for considering the key elements of resilience has been developed by an organisation called Robertson Cooper. They believe there are four key dimensions to resilience, as shown below.

A MODEL FOR RESILIENCE
ADAPTED FROM ROBERTSON COOPER

If we have *confidence* in our own abilities, this can really help us cope with stressful situations and come through them successfully. Of course, a little bit of self-doubt is healthy, but if we feel overwhelmed by what we are facing and don't believe we are good enough to cope with a particular challenge, then bouncing back can be hard.

Having access to great *social support* also really helps. Sometimes, just having someone to talk to about a setback can make us feel better. This person might be a colleague, but often it is someone at home or a trusted friend or family member. The important thing is recognising when we need to talk something through and then actually doing it.

Thirdly, when we are facing a setback, it can sometimes be necessary to take a different approach. If we just carry on as before, there is a real chance the same issue or problem will just appear again. Building our *adaptability*, how open or flexible we are to changing our approach, can really help.

Finally, and often crucially when it comes to recovering from a setback, is our *purposefulness*. If we really believe in what we are doing and really care about why it matters, this can help us get through difficult times. As Steve Radcliffe reminded us in Chapter 1, leaders who are 'up to something' really make things happen. This same passion for what we are doing can help us cope with what can sometimes seem like insurmountable obstacles or challenges.

Nudges

- How good are you at appreciating and managing your emotions?

- Are you able to stay optimistic, even in the most difficult circumstances?

- To what extent are you currently able to learn from your mistakes?

- Are you good at taking those difficult decisions and occasionally admitting publicly when you are wrong?

- Do you have the courage to take calculated risks, even if this sometimes involves going out on a limb?

- What are your strengths and potential areas for growth in the resilience model shared in this chapter?

Survey your scene

A few observations and much reasoning lead to error; many observations and a little reasoning to truth.

ALEXIS CARREL

Alexis Carrel was a French surgeon and biologist who was awarded the Nobel Prize in Physiology and Medicine in 1912. During World War 1, he served as a Major in the French Army Medical Corps and during this time helped devise the well known and widely used Carrel-Dakin method of treating war wounds.

Knowing your strengths and your potential areas for growth is powerful. But if you can combine this with a strong insight into your situation and the people around you, your ability to really make things happen can know no limits.

Understanding your context properly is crucial before you decide upon your priorities for action and your approach to implementation. How well do you know your operating context, whether that is a phase, a project area or team within a department, a whole business itself or a group of businesses? Working out your strategy must begin with where you are and what you need to do to get to where you want to go.

Performance data can tell you a lot about your context, particularly when the data is benchmarked against similar organisations in your industry. But there are many other sources of evidence you may want to consider, as performance data alone can present a narrow snapshot of context.

Many businesses use anonymous survey or questionnaire data to identify strengths and areas for development. If you are working in the public sector the majority of the tools available provide useful data on national averages that enable you to benchmark your current position. In the private sector many organisations are using social media as a method of constantly reviewing customer feedback to try and monitor their performance. At *Honk!* we have developed *Engage*, a tool that provides powerful feedback from staff, giving great insight into how levels of discretionary effort are improving over time.

But there is also no substitute for talking to as many people as you can at every opportunity and in a way that makes them feel at ease and free to say what they really think, which is a skill in itself. Apart from gleaning useful information, spending time talking to colleagues can also do a lot to increase engagement and discretionary effort, so long as people feel it has been a genuine process. Andy knows a number of headteachers who interviewed every single member of staff when they joined their school to find out what was working well and what would make the school even better. The impact on staff was universally positive – everyone likes to feel they have been heard. He even knows one head who, after more than 15 years in charge of the same school, still meets with every member of the teaching and support staff each year.

Nick Shopland, owner of the NJS Group, makes a point of visiting each and every construction site his company runs and will spend time listening to his people to make sure the decisions his management are making are understood and make sense to those who have to put them into action. Terry Leahy, CEO of Tesco in its purple years, spent at least a day a week on the floor of one of the supermarkets, listening to staff and customers. This is also a great way of discovering the rising stars within your team.

NICK SHOPLAND

TERRY LEAHY

Combining your evidence

The more you can triangulate your evidence, the more accurate a picture you can create of where you are on your journey.

Amanda Tucker, Head of Charitable Operations at Western Sussex NHS Foundation Trust, states that charities are of course always judged by their numbers and how much they have raised, yet in her

AMANDA TUCKER

opinion their success should also be judged by looking at the areas where the charity actually spends the money raised and the success of each project. In addition, the charity should be looking at who have been attracted as contributors and what impact the charity is having on the culture of the organisation it is supporting. She understands that these other features are sometimes hard to quantify but they are vital when making a call on how successful the organisation is in its work; 'As a charity, we provide awareness of issues and create a general feel-good factor to the general culture at the hospital trust that we support'.

Recognise what data you need to judge the performance of your organisation

Amanda also states that some aspects of the charity sector have had a bad reputation recently, and in parts deservedly so; 'Trust is in my opinion the most valuable commodity we have: our donors trust us with their often hard-earned cash; they trust us to ensure that the money they donate makes the biggest difference possible, helps the most people and is handled in the most professional way. We have to support our actions with proof of our actions.'

Of course, there will be an array of evidence to collect depending on your work. In the private sector this could be sales performance, customer satisfaction feedback, analysis of departments, individual appraisals, or management group performance to name a few. In the police this may relate to arrest rates, crime rates, crimes solved, or a public safety survey. The important point here is to recognise what data you need to judge the performance of your organisation. You can then create processes to collect this evidence, so you can use it to improve your performance at all levels in an ongoing cycle of improvement. Note that we come back to the importance of knowing your organisation: the more you know what it stands for, the more you can focus your research and target your systems to collect the right information.

We create a set of assumptions about the world around us

The ladder of inference

One of the reasons different individuals may come to different conclusions about the quality of the same information is that we all bring our own experiences and subconscious prejudices to bear, and these inevitably have an impact on how we interpret what we observe. We have a tendency to be selective when absorbing the information in front of us and on the basis of this partial picture, we create a set of assumptions about the world around us. These assumptions lead to us drawing conclusions about situations and ultimately creating a new set of beliefs. These in turn feed back to how we select data; usually whatever reinforces those sets of beliefs. In addition, our beliefs will tend to influence the actions we take, and this in turn leads us to turn our attention to certain sets of data, thus re-starting the whole process. This phenomenon is known as the ladder of inference and is summarised in the diagram below.

Put simply, leaders, senior managers and managers in any business or organisation are no different from anyone else – we are always at risk of making assumptions and jumping to conclusions. Developing the habit of taking time to properly understand situations, often through asking open questions and giving consideration to as wide a range of data and information as possible, can make a big difference to one's comprehension of them. Linked to this, inviting others to challenge our own perspectives, and thanking them when they do, is also an important habit in a leader. If others are afraid to challenge us as leaders, we run the risk of perpetuating our view of the world, which can lead to us losing touch with the reality of situations.

Amanda Tucker states: 'I always encourage my team to challenge my opinions so that we can make the most of every opportunity.'

The composite view of context

So, as well as understanding those around you, it is also critical to be clear about your wider context, taking into account as many sources of data and information as you can. Whatever level of leadership you are operating at, this will enable you to be even more effective at deciding what you need to do and how to go about doing it.

At The Key, Fergal and his team used to spend at least six weeks each year having a deep look at their strategy, and this would always start with an analysis of what was changing in the external environment and how well adapted The Key was to the way the world had changed. They would use two very well-known tools: SWOT and PESTLE.

SWOT

This simply represents Strengths, Weaknesses, Opportunities and Threats. At The Key, different mixed discipline teams would sit down over sandwiches at lunch time and have a think about where the company had got to. By having several different teams involved, you expand the perspective, thereby increasing the likelihood that you will capture a very full picture of where you are.

MIXED DISCIPLINE TEAMS WOULD SIT DOWN OVER SANDWICHES AT LUNCH TIME AND HAVE A THINK ABOUT WHERE THE COMPANY HAD GOT TO

Pundits would say that individuals should not think too hard before contributing. The points they make should be straight from the heart and not over-processed. No one should challenge anything that another member of the group has offered and every point should be given as much credence as the others. The aim here is simply to capture a range of thoughts that staff members have, based on their interaction with the organisation on a day-to-day basis.

One person will write up on the flip chart the points that are called out, without that person questioning the validity of what is being said. Go through all the strengths and then switch to the next heading. Alternatively, split up the team (if it is big) into twos or threes and get them to work separately on strengths, weaknesses, opportunities and threats then bring everything together for the whole group to look at and add to.

At The Key, there would be a project administrator who would pull together all the points made across all the teams and this would be given to the senior management team for further consideration as they assembled the strategy for the coming year.

Strengths

Where is the organisation strong? Where does it stand out from the crowd? Why? Where has it got stronger in the last year? What about its people – are they more skilled, more talented, more confident now? And products or outputs – in what way are they doing better than they were last year? Is the revenue higher, or the profit or surplus? What about the sustainability of the organisation? Are the systems and infrastructure better organised and more efficient than they were? If so, how? Is the organisation less prone to disaster because it is that much stronger? What about the pipeline of new work or revenue for the future? How guaranteed are the company revenues? If many more contracts have become three-year rather than one-year, or if your business development or sales team have many more leads (that pass the test of robustness) than they had last year, that could indicate a growing confidence in your brand. When it comes to retention rates, how are your client or customer numbers doing in comparison to last year? Has your retention rate gone up or at least been maintained? What about your costs? Are they going down as a percentage of turnover? Typically any company will expect to be getting more and more efficient each year. Have you managed to automate any jobs that should be done by computer rather than by a human? All of these things should be taken into account as you think about your strengths.

HAVE YOU MANAGED TO AUTOMATE ANY JOBS THAT SHOULD BE DONE BY COMPUTER RATHER THAN BY A HUMAN?

Weaknesses

Basically this is the flip side of strengths, where you try to identify those areas of the organisation where you are relatively less strong. Maybe you haven't been able to find the right person for a key role. Maybe a contract you thought was in the bag is now becoming a bit flakey. Maybe the new customer relations management software you have bought, at huge expense, has not been working properly. Maybe you haven't managed to sort out the lease on your property, and it's due to expire within six months. Perhaps the chair of your board has become ill and there is no obvious successor.

Could you use your skillset to extend the footprint of services you are currently offering your clients?

Opportunities

This is your chance to ask your staff what they think the organisation could be doing, as opposed to what it is doing right now. Is there an additional contract that could be won? Could you use your skillset to extend the footprint of services you are currently offering your clients? Could you acquire or merge with another organisation that would greatly extend your scope, get you noticed more and offer the chance of cost efficiencies? Maybe there is a brilliant person you have met, who could transform your business information team, who you think may be willing to join the organisation, if only you can afford them.

Threats

This is where you have to think really negatively, put on your depressed hat and articulate all the ways in which your organisation is not safe. Typically such a consideration will focus heavily on competitors, or changes in customer or client behaviour. Some of the points made under the PESTLE heading below will fit into this category.

PESTLE

FRANCIS AGUILAR

Harvard professor Francis Aguilar is thought to be the creator of PEST Analysis. He included a scanning tool called ETPS in his 1967 book, *Scanning the Business Environment*. The name was later tweaked to create the current acronym, PESTLE. There are many different ways of using it, but at The Key, teams would consider the environment from the following perspectives:

Politically

What is happening in national and local government that could have an impact on the success of the organisation? What if the government changed and the new administration was against public sector organisations outsourcing to other organisations? What if all local authorities set up their own enterprise arms to trade the services they traditionally offered for free? Would that create a huge competitive challenge?

Economically

What is happening in regard to the ability of our customers to pay for the products we are selling to them? What about the cost for us in employing staff? Is national insurance going up? What about the contributions we have to make to personal pensions – how will that change in the coming year? What about the corporate tax situation?

How can we adapt working hours to suit the way staff want to work

Socially

We mainly employ millennials, who want a strong sense of purpose, sensible hours and lots of flexibility in how they work, so what can we do to attract and retain them? What can we do to increase agile working, so people can work at different offices, or from home with total ease? How can we adapt working hours to suit the way staff want to work, without compromising the service we offer our clients? We know that the latest research says that performance feedback is far more effective if it is given regularly, as things happen, rather than waiting for the annual review. How do we need to adapt our approach to fit in with that? What should we do about training?

Technologically

We know that more and more managers are accessing information from their smart phones rather than their desktops. So, how are we adapting our provision accordingly? People are spending less time reading text, and we know they are not scrolling down an article as much as they were. We therefore need to consider how we can get the main points to come as early in the article as possible, if we are to respond to our clients' behaviour. Moving our hosting into the cloud would save us huge costs, but is it as secure? What can we do?

Legally

With huge changes in how we are legally obliged to manage people's personal information, to what extent are our systems optimised in order to guarantee that we will be compliant, without adding huge cost? We have issues around office space, are we allowed, under our current lease, to let out part of the office to another organisation? If we can't, then what's the plan?

Environmentally

The cycle to work scheme, which is hugely advantageous to those buying bikes and equipment to travel into work, has very little take up. What can we do to change people's attitudes? We are still printing far too much, how can we minimise this? The government is offering a range of measures to encourage companies to adapt how they are working, to what extent are we taking full advantage of these? What do we need to do to change?

Lag and lead indicators

At The Key people talked a lot about lag indicators and lead indicators. *Lag* refers to what has happened in the past and we worked hard to understand trends in every area of company operation, from revenue to costs to average length of employment over time, so we could become more efficient and effective. But *lead* indicators refer to anything that gives you a sense of what might be coming in the future. It may be a conversation you overhear at a conference, or something you have read in a news article. Or it might be your own combined analysis of what you think is happening in the environment.

Fergal had the sense that people running schools would come more and more to accept that they operated in the wider world of managing organisations in the same way as people in other sectors, and that as a consequence The Key should offer more and more insight for school leaders from well beyond the world of education. This was based on seeing more and more school leaders doing MBAs, more focus being put on business people joining the boards of academies and the language of business being adopted more universally in the school system.

Another lead indicator might be a conversation in the kitchen with someone who has suggested to a colleague that they aren't happy. That should feed back to the leadership, who will want to address the situation and ensure they do not lose a valuable member of staff. Another might be that customer renewals in one particular segment of your client base appear to have dropped off for a month. Could that indicate there will be a weakening of renewals in the future? If so, could that spread to other segments? Ensuring that you focus hard on lead indicators will keep your organisation in the real world, ready and primed for what might be coming around the corner. Sadly, many companies ignore them: think about Blockbuster or AOL or Woolworths. A failure to spot changes in the environment led to their sad demise.

Why monitoring matters

Monitoring within a team, company or organisation enables you, at any point in time, to know where things are. It's how you know about the deal your customers, stakeholders and shareholders are getting, and is a way of properly understanding your culture.

There are several approaches to monitoring you can implement and the more you link them together, the more accurate the results will be.

Just walking around will give you an idea of where each department is in terms of the activity and the feel of the environment itself. Management by Walking Around (MBWA) is a well-trodden approach to monitoring in business, particularly promulgated by Sir John Harvey-Jones, who was chairman of ICI in the 1980s and fronted the popular BBC TV series *Troubleshooter* in the 90s. These walks tend to fall on a spectrum from formal to less so, and can be timed at irregular intervals to give a more rounded picture of the business. Quick, ten-minute meetings with individuals can really help you get to know your team members. These should be focused, and the information gathered can be used in the wider context of team meetings to set plans and agendas for the week or month ahead.

At team meetings KPIs can be scrutinised, sales can be discussed, and customer feedback analysed. The key point here is that you can ensure everybody is well synchronised in terms of focus and targets. No doubt your company or organisation will have its own set of working practices which should be tested from time to time for their efficacy.

However it is organised in practice, there are some fundamentals about monitoring to consider:

- Everyone involved needs to accept the approach and buy in to the idea of how it is being done.

- Ensure everyone knows exactly why monitoring is so important and that the outcome will contribute to performance improvement.

- What can people expect in the form of feedback? How often will it happen and what will they be expected to do with it?

You and your colleagues need to follow an agreed approach so you deliver a consistent, fair and helpful monitoring process.

> Ensure everyone knows exactly why monitoring is so important and that the outcome will contribute to performance improvement

A key consideration with all monitoring is how you get the balance right between assuring yourself that things are as they should be, and not making colleagues feel like you don't trust them. In the end, this comes down to your own professional judgement, based on reliable information on both performance and morale. Fergal used regular staff surveys via Survey Monkey at The Key, always trying not to prejudice the information he gathered with his own preconceptions.

Using data

It's a bit of a cliché but as the adage suggests, continually weighing a pig doesn't make it any fatter. Or, plant the daffodil bulb and let it grow; don't keep digging it up to see how it's doing. Critics think some organisations spend too much time and energy measuring anything that moves at the expense of concentrating on getting on with the job in hand and focusing on service delivery. Indeed, there are organisations like the NHS, the police or schools that spend a lot of time collecting all kinds of data that has negligible impact on patient care, solving crimes or pupils' learning outcomes. Tables and tables of information sitting on a marvellous database do little in themselves to drive up standards, but understandably organisations are pressured by government departments who have to justify the spending of public money to the electorate.

Farmers, however, would argue otherwise. There will always be a need to weigh a pig from time to time to make sure there is nothing wrong with it. It ought to be gaining weight at a certain rate – if it isn't, then why not? Monitoring the pig's weight allows the farmer to intervene

PLANT THE DAFFODIL BULB AND LET IT GROW; DON'T KEEP DIGGING IT UP TO SEE HOW IT'S DOING if there is a problem. It allows the farmer to reflect on what works best and what doesn't seem to be working. It allows the farmer to try out new ideas and evaluate whether they are successful.

In other words, when it comes to data, you need to model yourself on the farming profession. You need to know how well staff are progressing and your team need to have data that will help them reflect on what is working and what is not. They need to be able to intervene when an individual or a part of the business appears to be falling behind. They also need to be able to see the overall big picture. Are there changes that need to be made to the current strategy or direction of your company or organisation?

Basing actions on out-of-date data is a waste of everyone's time and will fail to secure buy-in from staff or team members

What is important here is the accuracy of the data, the frequency with which it is collected, and the day-to-day analysis that leads to timely and focused planning. Such planning will only be effective if data is current, has been collected efficiently and is accurate. For example, it's very important when judging sales figures to be looking at like-for-like figures. Basing actions on out-of-date data is a waste of everyone's time and will fail to secure buy-in from staff or team members. Hopefully your organisation will have all this in hand. If colleagues are telling you otherwise, maybe it is time to look again at how you organise your data processes. The Supper Club, an organisation of entrepreneurs that Fergal belongs to, constantly advises its members, almost all of whom are CEOs and bosses, to work *on* the business rather than *in* the business. You have to get perspective to be able to see what is actually going on. You are constantly forming a meta-narrative via a lens that is at arm's length from the day-to-day operation of the organisation.

Whatever the practicalities of the process, accuracy is critical. This means it is essential that you have robust systems for moderating staff evaluations, both through work scrutiny and appraisal. For middle managers in particular, regularly allocating time to this in meetings – where it is possible – is a useful way of making sure everyone is working to the same set of expectations about what constitutes a particular grade or level. Some teams find it helpful to keep portfolios of work as part of the evidence that can support this approach.

Nudges

- Do you or colleagues use anonymous survey data from customers, staff, management and stakeholders to regularly assess the culture and climate of your workplace?

- How do you monitor the work of your staff and their performance? Are the systems you have established at a whole-business level being robustly and transparently implemented?

- How are you using the evidence collected to build your business and improve your performance?

- Do you have a good balance and breadth of monitoring approaches?

- Do you use the data you collect about staff progress in a way that supports their learning?

- How do you know the data you collect is accurate?

- Would there be any benefit in doing this more collaboratively?

Know your team

The key to realising a dream is to focus not on success but on significance, and then even the small steps and little victories along your path will take on greater meaning.

OPRAH WINFREY

Oprah Winfrey was born in Kosciusko, Mississippi in 1954. In 1976, she moved to Baltimore, where she hosted a hit TV chat show. A Chicago TV station recruited her to host their morning show, and she later presented her own, wildly popular programme, *The Oprah Winfrey Show*, which aired for 25 seasons, from 1986 to 2011.

The better you know the people you work with, the better you will be able to bring out the best in them, adjusting your individual approach with each person to suit what they need from you.

Just like you, your colleagues will all have their own predispositions, strengths and areas for growth. But do you know what these are? Do you consciously and deliberately think about your approach with the individuals you interact with and reflect on those differences? Or do you just tend to work with everyone the same way, in line with your own preferences, rather than what is going to get the best out of them? This can work to a degree, but long term it can also be an easy trap to get stuck in; once you stop asking questions, you risk no longer getting the best out of people.

Using personality tools and 360 surveys can be helpful, which is why we created honk.org.uk to give low-cost access to the power of simple diagnostic tools.

There is also huge potential to understand colleagues from your day-to-day interactions with them, whether you are a middle manager, senior manager or running a company or group of companies. There will be key people at work whom you would benefit from getting to know and understand well, including those who report to you, your peers and others who may be more senior, such as board members and other stakeholders. So how do you make the most of these interactions?

At its heart, your approach needs to focus on taking the time and effort to listen to and observe colleagues carefully. The assertion from Mehrabian (1972) that only 7% of communication comes from what is said, while 38% is through tone of voice and 55% from reading body language is a helpful reminder that we need to be attuned to all three aspects of communication. It can be useful to develop the habit that Chapter 19 of this book will develop in much more detail: that of *asking first*. By asking neutral questions, you can establish much more quickly where someone is with their thinking or level of motivation on an issue.

What are you looking for?

In simple terms, leaders need to try to understand others' competence, preferred ways of working and their motivations. If you can work these out, you are in a position to tailor your approach accordingly. When you are introducing a new idea, some colleagues will need to understand how it fits into the wider strategy before you get into the detail. Others will need to understand the detail of how something is going to work in practice before they are interested in its place within the wider strategy. Factor this thinking into your approach in order to increase buy-in to your ideas and engagement from colleagues.

Some of your team will be much happier if you have a clear implementation plan already mapped out so they can see the way ahead is organised and decided. For others, this matters much less, with some colleagues preferring not to have too much tied down too soon, in case flexibility with ongoing implementation is compromised. Our online tool, *Persona*, available on the *Honk!* website, is an easy way to develop this wider understanding of your colleagues. Of course, it helps you as a leader if you understand your own preferred style and how best to adapt this to certain individuals or groups.

PERSONA

Playing to strengths

One other key reason for getting to know your team well is to find out what they are good at and make sure you and your colleagues take the opportunity to play to their strengths. In her article *The incomplete leader*, Deborah Ancona (2007) argues that the very best leaders know what it is they are good at and find other people to lead on the areas where they are not as strong. Apart from this making sense at the most basic level, it is also an approach that builds individuals' levels of motivation for two reasons: firstly, because you or a colleague has identified their strength in the first place; and secondly, because we all like doing things we are good at. So, from every perspective, make sure you not only have the right people on the bus, but also that they are sitting in the right seats.

In their book *Leadership: all you need to know*, Pendleton and Furnham (2012) have taken this thinking and created a simple but effective model for considering how to take into account both the performance of colleagues and their natural predispositions.

PLAYING TO STRENGTHS
ADAPTED FROM PENDLETON AND FURNHAM (2012)

For areas where an individual has *natural strengths*, it's important to give them the chance to excel and continue developing, with the aim of becoming even better and the go-to person within your team or organisation for that area.

Potential strengths are those areas which, with just a little attention, a colleague could be great at. This is generally because they have a predisposition towards it and just need to give it some focus.

Fragile strengths are things that an individual can do well if they put their mind to it, but success in these areas doesn't come easily. For example, all managers need to be able to use data effectively. For some, this will be a natural strength. For others, it takes practice and focus. But it is achievable.

In contrast, what the model calls *resistant limitations* are those things an individual isn't good at and frankly has no interest or motivation to try to improve. We have heard this described as the thing that was in your school report that still seems to come up in your annual appraisal now. Pendleton and Furnham argue that rather than continue year after year to make this a focus for development, one is much better trying to find a workaround, which usually involves finding someone else to do it.

However, there are some things one simply cannot delegate to someone else, like managing relationships and how you behave with your team

The more senior one is, the easier it is to play to one's own strengths and delegate tasks that play to colleagues' strengths, as Ancona argues one should. This should work at all levels if you monitor your situation regularly. We must sound a note of caution, however, as there are some things one simply cannot delegate to someone else, like managing relationships and how you behave with your team. Making excuses and not taking responsibility for your actions in this area can be self-destructive and should be avoided at all costs. In the end, there must be a decent fit between an individual and their role. If this is missing, then it's not good news for the individual or your team.

Managing differential performance in others

As well as knowing about how others prefer to work and playing to their strengths, the very best leaders in any organisation or business, at all levels, know how well colleagues in their team are performing, and respond accordingly. Pendleton and Furnham (2012) developed a model which suggests leaders can group colleagues according to their behaviours and values and their performance at work.

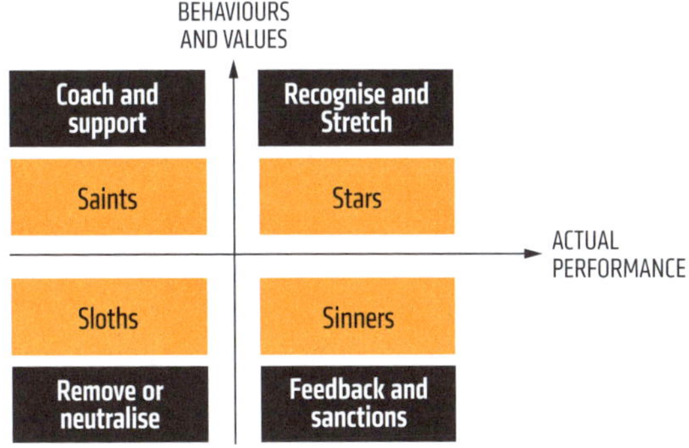

PERFORMANCE AND BEHAVIOURS
ADAPTED FROM PENDLETON AND FURNHAM (2012)

Let's begin with the stars. These are your high performers who are doing a great job and work in a way that is absolutely in line with the culture and climate you wish to create. They are also the group you need to be careful not to overlook or take for granted. Just like you, your stars need to be challenged, stretched and recognised for what they do. The more they feel they have a say in their future, the better, but you need to make sure you don't over promise. They will usually appreciate development opportunities, whether formal or informal. They may also be useful when it comes to coaching others, particularly your saints, and would make great mentors for your newcomers. Remember to consider them in the context of succession planning.

Just like you, your stars need to be challenged, stretched and recognised for what they do

At the other extreme are your sloths. These are individuals who are performing poorly and are potentially having a pernicious effect on your culture and climate. You quickly need to understand what sits behind their poor outcomes and attitude and give them very clear and unambiguous feedback about what needs to change in relation to both. Make it clear they are making choices about their future. They need to improve rapidly or there will be consequences. Ultimately, if there is no great improvement, work out a way for them to leave fast but with dignity.

Your saints are well-meaning members of your team, but they are just not particularly effective. As with the sloths, you need to take time to understand what is stopping them from doing a good job and then make sure they are supported and coached to improve. As long as they continue to improve at a sufficient rate, you should continue to support them. Be aware that these people can take up a disproportionate amount of time so keep an eye on that. Only if they seem to have peaked at a point which is below your expectations should you consider how they might also move on to pastures new.

Your sinners need to be given very clear feedback as to what needs to change and by when

Finally, the toughest group of all are your sinners. These are high performing individuals who get great results and achieve strongly, but do it in a way that undermines the culture and climate you are trying to establish. They don't, for example get work done on time or follow organisational systems properly. They are often disloyal about your leadership and others in the wider team. In short, they are an annoying thorn in your side. If you have inherited a team whose performance across the board is poor, you may decide you have to live with your sinners for a while, as having *anyone* who is performing might be a priority. You've identified them, so maybe use them to your advantage for a while. But if, over time, it feels like you have reached a tipping point where their negative effect on the wider team is exceeding the positive impact of their own performance, take action. Unlike the saints, who need coaching, your sinners need to be given very clear feedback as to what needs to change and by when. Remember, a sinner can perform, so reminding them strongly of your expectations may be enough to get them to respond positively. Coaching probably isn't what's needed. They just need to decide to change or to face the consequences. Ultimately, they may need to leave too, if changes don't occur.

Most organisations or businesses are better at dealing with saints than sinners, partly as there is usually much more written down about the levels of competence that need to be achieved and partly because they are usually easier characters to deal with. But having clear statements of expectations regarding behaviours is equally important if one is to tackle what, for sinners, are more likely to be disciplinary issues than those relating to competence.

I don't think Pendleton and Furnham are suggesting you should put each of your staff into one of the boxes and label them in this rather black and white way, as people are more complex than that. But the model provides a useful way for you to think about how different individuals may need different specific approaches rather than a general response to any given situation, regardless of context. You may find that mapping your team is a useful way of identifying who sits in which category; over time you can follow their progress and see if they move from group to group.

The final part of this chapter gives some practical strategies that might be useful when thinking about your team. These are suggestions, again from Pendleton and Furnham, as to what might be worth considering in each area.

YOU MAY FIND THAT MAPPING YOUR TEAM IS A USEFUL WAY OF IDENTIFYING WHO SITS IN WHICH CATEGORY; OVER TIME YOU CAN FOLLOW THEIR PROGRESS AND SEE IF THEY MOVE FROM GROUP TO GROUP

Stars

- Biggest challenge is keeping them motivated, engaged, progressing
- Make sure they know they are recognised and valued
- Careful, selective feedback
- Involve them in setting their own goals to a greater extent
- Understand their career goals and commit to supporting them
- Delegate more responsibility – enlarge their role, special projects
- Give them exposure to more senior colleagues
- Offer them the opportunity to represent the group or team
- Invite them to coach and develop others in the team, such as the saints or newcomers
- They need clear, unambiguous expectations about career progression – don't promise what you can't deliver
- Don't ever take them for granted

Saints

- Find out what the cause of the underperformance is
- They may not understand expectations or goals
- Don't have skills or haven't learned them yet
- Lack of motivation
- Don't realise they are not delivering – have received no feedback
- Wrong fit for the job
- Something in their private life
- Give feedback – specific, examples relevant, timely
- Coaching, training, development
- Support and buddying, for example from a star
- Re-define the job responsibilities
- Set short term goals and give frequent feedback
- Get them to take ownership
- Keep track of actions and performance discussions

Sinners

- Find out the underlying cause (arrogance, boredom, don't care)
- Confront the behaviour assertively, explain the impact on others, hold the mirror up
- Beware of the impact of tolerating poor behaviour and values on the rest of the team and colleagues
- Get them to own their behaviour and the impact on others
- Explain that behaviour and values are part of how their performance is judged, not just their results
- A few clear rules and boundaries
- Make sure they commit to specific changes
- Make sure they own the action plan
- Challenge them to become a star
- Connect the behaviour or attitude with something they care about
- Peer pressure
- Consequences for not changing – get them to accept it is in their hands – it's their choice
- Keep track of actions and performance discussions
- Be prepared to move them on if you judge the negative impact on the team or organisation outweighs the positive

Sloths

- Act fast with a quick diagnosis of underlying causes as per saints and sinners, decide if it is primarily a skill, motivation or attitude problem – employ the same tactics as for saints or sinners
- Feedback, feedback, feedback
- Clear communication of expectation of improvement; if not, consequences
- Get them to own the plan
- Be clear about how long you will give them to turn things around
- Keep track of actions and performance discussions
- Be prepared to fire them if they don't improve fast

Nudges

- How well do you know your team?

- How do you support colleagues to play to their strengths?

- To what extent do you enable team members to work on the right areas?

- Are you open to helping to find workarounds where they seem appropriate?

- Do you understand others' personality predispositions? Do you use any personality tools to support this?

- Do you use 360 reviews or other mechanisms to better understand the performance of others around you?

- How good are you at really focusing on what others are saying or what their tone of voice and body language is telling you?

- How well do you deliberately play to others' strengths?

- How good are you at consciously differentiating the way you work with colleagues who display different behaviours or levels of performance?

Be up to something

STEVE RADCLIFFE

Steve Radcliffe is one of Europe's top leadership experts. In the last 20 years, he has provided leadership coaching to over 50 chief executives and heads of the Civil Service, the NHS and other government departments.

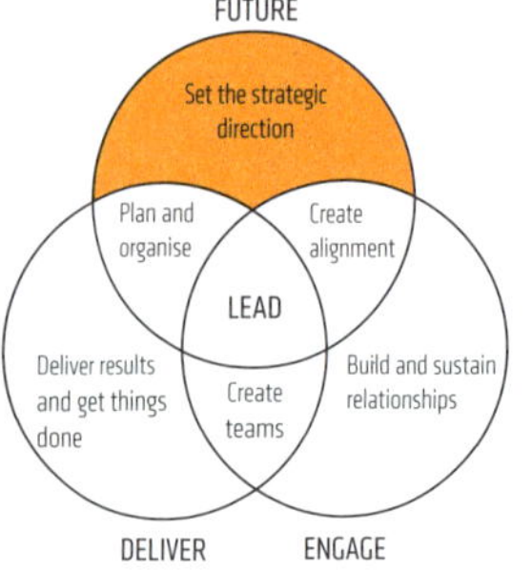

If you know what you want to achieve with your team or organisation, and what you are passionate about, you will be able to focus your efforts, build a shared vision for the future and really make things happen.

An organisation or company needs at its core to know what they stand for and what they want to achieve.

This may be expressed in very simple terms such as ensuring a business does its utmost to help every customer as much as it can. But in the very best companies there is also a vision for the special ingredients in the context of the business that go towards making it a success. At *Honk!* we like this definition: 'A vision statement is an aspirational description of what an organisation would like to achieve or accomplish in the mid-term or long-term future. It is intended to serve as a clear guide to choosing current and future courses of action.'

It's common sense that successful organisations and companies will have a similar attitude to their vision statement, but you'd be surprised how many from both the public and private sectors can struggle with this.

A vision statement is an aspirational description of what an organisation would like to achieve or accomplish in the mid-term or long-term future

Start with why

One very powerful way of thinking about this has been suggested by Simon Sinek in his best-selling book: *Start with why* (2011).

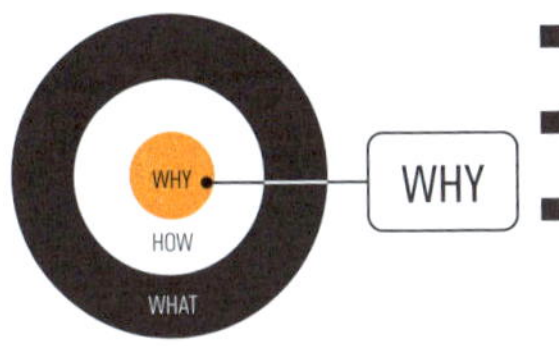

- Our driving purpose (**mission**)
- What we believe and care about (**values**)
- Our high-level goals and why they matter (**vision**)

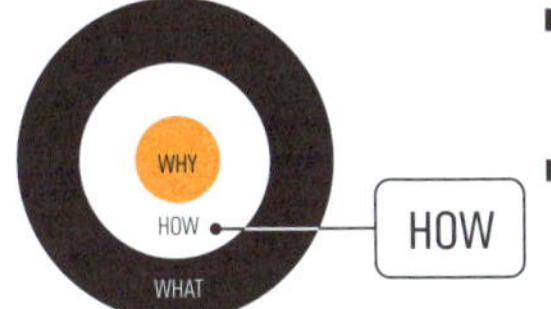

- The strategic approaches that enable us to achieve what really matters to us: our WHY
- Usually, one broad approach or strategy for each-level high goal

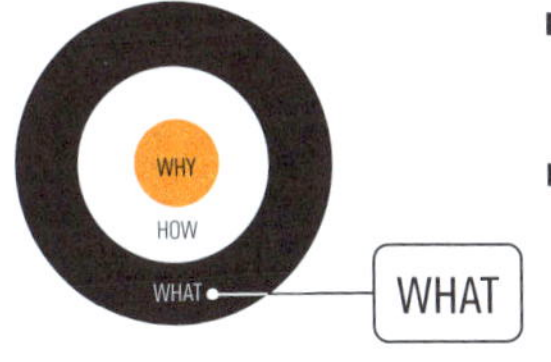

- The actions or plans that we implement to achieve out HOW
- The individual, team and organisational routines,processes and habits that deliver success

START WITH WHY
SIMON SINEK (2011)

Sinek argues that most organisations can describe *what* they do, some can articulate *how* they do what they do, and very few know *why* they do what they do. He believes the best organisations turn this on its head and start from the inside out, by thinking about the *why* first. Those in the public sector, the NHS or the police for example, have a huge advantage in this respect; the reasons you come to work and the reasons your organisation exists are well understood and important for everyone in your profession. If, on the other hand, your focus is exclusively on profit growth, these core reasons can sometimes get lost. Taking time to consider properly the way in which we seek to achieve success is where the importance of the *how* – the strategy – emerges, and *what* we actually do follows from there.

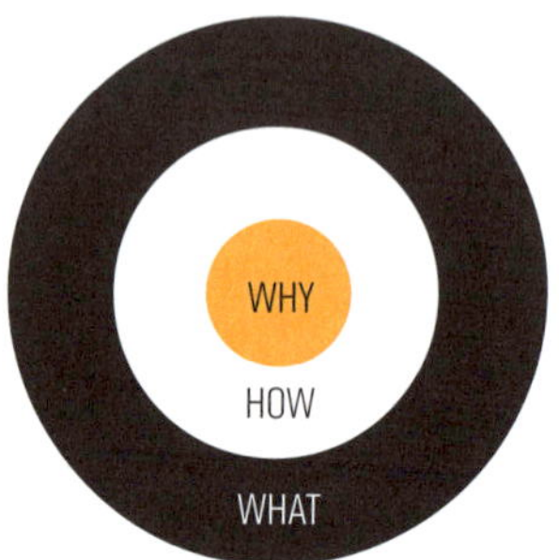

APPLYING THE *START WITH WHY* MODEL IN PRACTICE

So how do organisations or companies go about arriving at their own mission, vision, values and strategy? From an individual perspective, your education and your early experiences through your career may have shaped your view of what an ideal organisation should look like, how it should feel and, importantly, how it might work. Almost unconsciously, senior leaders know what they want to achieve, but translating these aspirations into words can be far from easy.

A shared sense of direction is vital in any organisation's success

There is also the question of how much the vision should only reflect the views of the senior leadership team or board. There is no doubt that the more people are involved in the process of defining an organisation's vision, including managers and staff, the greater the sense of ownership and buy-in. You'd be surprised how motivating this can be for the next generation if they know they have a say.

So, a shared sense of direction is vital in any organisation's success. However, consultation of this kind comes with a strong health warning and needs skillful handling by leaders. The last thing one wants to end up with is a series of bland statements that could apply to any business, which everyone agrees with, but which don't really end up saying anything distinctive. And a further note of caution here, be aware that too many voices can muddy the water and your key words can get lost.

Your vision must be *your* vision and must be specific to what you do.

This challenge is magnified when you have a group of companies. If you are a group leader, you will no doubt recognise the tension between allowing each company its own identity and ensuring that your group of companies can define its distinctive qualities. One way to square this circle, which draws on the giraffe concept mentioned in Chapter 1, is for a group of companies to define together its key principles (the long neck issues) and then allow each company to interpret and refine these in their own context (the markings).

Devising strategy

A strategy is a long-term plan for the whole organisation or company. Igor Ansoff, a Russian-born American mathematician and business thinker, defined corporate strategy as 'The positioning and relating of the organisation to its environment in a way which will assure its continued success and make it safe from surprises.' He devised a mathematical grid setting out the possibilities available to an organisation for generating economic growth: offering new products, improving existing products, improving penetration of existing markets, and developing new markets. For your organisation, working out the right strategic mix is likely to be important.

IGOR ANSOFF

THE ANSOFF MODEL

Of course, there are many theoretical approaches out there, but here are eight key types of strategy that most organisations or companies are involved with at any given time, regardless of their size.

1. *Growth* involves the expansion of a business, its markets, products, and size. Successful growth strategies are based on having the

resources to support growth, identifying the markets that make growth worthwhile and being better than the competition in these growth markets.

2. *Stability* involves a consolidation strategy for the organisation, often before a period of growth. The organisation needs a stable base with clear procedures and systems during this period, before moving on.

3. *Profitability* is an important part of business and one which is sometimes forgotten, it is particularly important in organisations where shareholders need a strong return on their investment.

4. *Efficiency* is concerned with how well limited resources have been used in meeting organisational objectives.

5. *Market leadership* strategies are all about being number one in your specific sector or vertical (a group of purchasers within that sector). Fergal's previous company, The Key, is the market leader, for instance, in the provision of professional knowledge and information to school leaders and governors. Being the market leader gives considerable cost advantages over rivals because other companies will have a smaller market share and therefore fewer opportunities for economies of scale.

> Being the market leader gives considerable cost advantages over rivals because other companies will have a smaller market share and therefore fewer opportunities for economies of scale

6. *Survival* is an obvious business goal. In a highly competitive business environment, survival is the baseline consideration for most organisations. When Fergal's company lost its government funding, survival was not guaranteed. He and his team had to bootstrap it into profit over a period of three years, meaning that the organisation had to exist without external help or capital. Once the profit came, the team could expand its horizons.

7. *Merger and acquisition* strategies enable businesses to benefit from the advantages of integration.

8. *Globalisation* strategies involve expanding internationally by developing manufacturing, distribution or sales facilities in other countries. For example, companies like Coca-Cola and McDonald's have moved into China and other new emerging markets. Product market

development involves firms maintaining their existing markets but developing new product markets within them.

Objective – strategy – tactics

In his 2015 book *Winners*, Alastair Campbell, the former director of communications for Tony Blair, talks about the importance of using OST: objective – strategy – tactics. His main point is that once you have an objective, it is important to consider what your main single strategy is for achieving it. He reflects on the 1997 UK general election. Their objective: for Labour to win the election. The strategy: we are *New* Labour. The tactics: a whole series of actions and policies that fitted the overall strategy, such as the removal of Clause Four, making friends with the right-wing press (Rupert Murdoch, in particular) and a new party logo. Outcome: they won the election. Contrast this with Labour's approach to the election in 2010 and you can see how there wasn't really an overall game plan. Yes, the objective was clear: regain power. But the tactics didn't add up to a coherent strategy. In fact, some of the policies and messaging seemed contradictory. For example, the party was at pains to point out that Labour 'is a friend of business' and 'the economy is safe with us.' Yet at the same time, they were advocating a cap on both energy prices and rents in private sector housing, suggesting they were anything but well-disposed to business.

ALASTAIR CAMPBELL

The critical point here is that, for any given objective, you should ideally aim for only one overall strategy and then line up your tactics underneath this. Nick Shopland says: 'Sticking to your plan is probably one of the toughest things to do, especially when you are starting out as a small to medium size business. You need to know what your business is about. There are so many distractions that if you are not careful you can lose your direction, time and most importantly money. Of course, you have to be aware of new opportunities and ideas, but they must be part of what you do. I wish that somebody had told me this when I started out.' Rob spent some time working with Nick and his team and they recognised the need to keep a clear vision, especially in a time of rapid growth. Nick often refers to the road map idea, where you have a set starting point and you know where you are going and where you are on your journey, all the while trying to avoid as many road bumps or detours as you can along the way. Like any map, there is always more than one way to get to your destination, but Nick says that in his opinion it's still best to 'take the shortest possible route and keep it simple, repeating it over and over again.'

Honk! supports this view, we see that the most successful organisations are those that work out a successful strategy and stick to it, making sure it is followed day in and day out, while having a clarity around a core purpose, simply expressed. Even the few words that make up the vision and mission statements of the average organisation can speak volumes, providing something to unite around.

The most successful organisations are those that work out a successful strategy and stick to it

As an example, one school Andy worked with recently has developed very clear and simple guidelines for all aspects of the school day. There are three key statements that underpin all the school does and can be applied to any situation by staff or pupils: 'The street stops at the gate', 'A relentless focus on high standards' and 'There are no barriers or excuses to great learning or achievement'.

Without this clear sense of where an organisation or company is meant to be going, there is a strong likelihood that it simply goes nowhere. Managers, middle managers and staff cannot operate with hundreds of policies circulating around their brains. They need clarity around a set of key principles which underpin the way things are expected to happen, and when they are not sure about something they can refer back to these principles and apply them appropriately.

It is this clarity that breeds trust and confidence

The same applies to any multi-layered company with leadership at different levels. When decisions need to be made by leaders in a department, there is nothing more helpful than clear guidance, a clear steer about how they should be made. It is this clarity that breeds trust and confidence within your community. It is also what gives senior and middle leaders the platform on which to make decisions within their own sphere of influence, knowing they will be in line with the overall strategic approach but flexed according to their context and circumstances. In other words, once again, it's the giraffe concept in action.

At The Key, Fergal and his team were very clear about what they wanted in terms of their objective: The Key would be considered the most effective and efficient tool in a school leader's toolkit. The strategy was to find every way possible to make their products indispensable, so that school managers would feel negligent for not using them on a day-to-day basis. The tactics were to strengthen brand recognition to increase awareness, provide products that took maximum pain away from school leaders whenever needed for the lowest cost possible, and build strong advocacy for The Key in every area of the sector.

Nudges

- Are you clear about exactly what you are trying to achieve and the two or three key elements of your work that will enable you to achieve it?

- Are board members, owners or trustees at the heart of the development of your strategic approach and the monitoring of its implementation and impact?

- Is the concept of OST (objective – strategy – tactics) something that might be useful for you to adopt in your context?

- Are you good at rejecting initiatives that may distract you from your focus?

- Are you clear about your core principles and do you set the highest expectations in all aspects of your work?

Stop; think; then decide

MICHELLE OBAMA
American writer, lawyer, and university administrator who served as
the First Lady of the United States from 2009 to 2017.

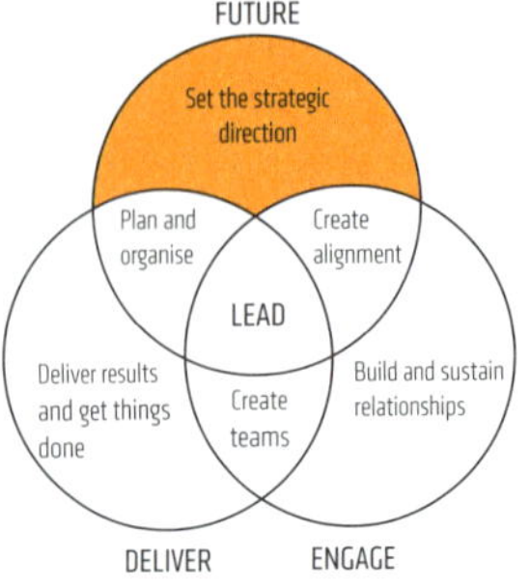

ANGELA MERKEL

Making good decisions is fundamental to any team or organisation's success. But we are not always as good at deciding stuff as we like to think we are. Developing your decision making abilities can really make a difference.

Leaders at all levels are making decisions every day. One of the world's great political leaders in recent times is Angela Merkel, whose academic background as a PhD graduate in quantum chemistry highlights her preference for gathering information and approaching problems scientifically. She is known for taking time to make calculated decisions based on each specific situation. She is also known for being open to making course corrections when executing plans. Her upbringing in East Germany has informed her leadership

decision making. As someone who grew up isolated in the Eastern Bloc, Merkel is a champion for tearing down walls, for openness and inclusivity, and this is evident in her stand on the refugee issue that Europe is currently dealing with.

Depending on the situation and with time permitting, it's important to use all the available resources to diagnose the problem, discuss causal factors with colleagues, ask them for options, consider the pros and cons, agree actions and review afterwards. The review stage is important, but often missed out. Allow time for asking: 'Was it the right decision? Is a different option now required? Has the situation changed? What did we learn from the action we took? What will we do if this happens again?'

Thinking fast and slow

Some of our decisions are made almost without thinking. We rely on our intuition and experience to tell us what we need to do. The psychologist Daniel Kahneman, in his book *Thinking fast and slow* (2011) calls these types of decisions 'system one' decisions. These are made automatically; when you turn around because there has been a loud bang behind you, you are doing it instinctively. You aren't consciously thinking, 'I wonder what that is, let's have a look.'

DANIEL KAHNEMAN

'System two' decisions are more rational. This is when you stop, take a moment to consider the situation, weigh up your options and then make your decision as to how to act. The figure below summarises these two different approaches.

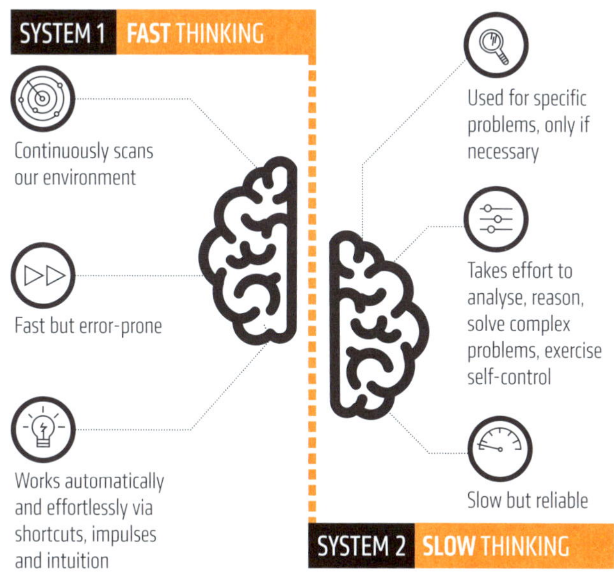

SYSTEM ONE AND TWO DECISION MAKING
KAHNEMAN (2011)

Understanding your decision making bias

An important element of system two thinking is making the right decisions based on the available evidence. So, if you systematically and routinely take this into account, making decisions should be straightforward. The trouble is, it's *not* that simple. There are various reasons why we don't make logical decisions, even when we try to. Psychologists point to several factors that can influence us without us even knowing. The most common types of decision making bias we all have the potential to demonstrate are shown below.

BIAS	DEFINITION
Anchoring	The tendency to rely too heavily, or *anchor*, on a past reference or on one trait or piece of information when making decisions.
Availability heuristic	Estimating what is more likely by what is more available in memory, which is biased towards vivid, unusual, or emotionally charged examples.
Endowment effect	The fact that people often demand much more to give up an object than they would be willing to pay to acquire it. Also connected with the *status quo* bias.
Framing effect	Drawing different conclusions from the same information, depending on how that information is presented.
Gambler's fallacy	The tendency to think that future probabilities are altered by past events, when in reality they are unchanged.
Group think	Peer pressure to conform to the opinions held by the group.
Optimism	The tendency to be over-optimistic, over-estimating favourable and pleasing outcomes.

COMMON TYPES OF DECISION MAKING BIAS
SOURCE: Q-LEARNING (2014)

Research indicates that bias tends to operate more in certain situations than others. Knowing when you are inherently more likely to be subject to an unconscious bias can help reduce the chances of making poor decisions. The three most common situations when bias is likely to kick in are described below.

Knowing when you are inherently more likely to be subject to an unconscious bias can help reduce the chances of making poor decisions

BIAS	SITUATION
i^+	**When there is lots of information** ✓ We notice or think of memorable items ✓ We notice when things have changed ✓ We remember the things we like
i^-	**When there isn't much information** ✓ We create patterns or simplify even when there is little data ✓ We fill in the gaps with our stereotypes ✓ We tend to focus on the things we know about or like more
$\bigcirc^-$	**When we need to act fast** ✓ Over-confident ✓ Favour things that we can do straight away ✓ Better the devil we know

When does bias tend to occur?

When it comes to making good decisions, we have come up with the very simple STOP model outlined below. If leaders just take a moment to stop and think about any given decision and run through the four stages of STOP, however briefly, it can help increase the chances of a favourable outcome.

The STOP model

Situation

Have you properly understood the situation? What additional information would it be useful to acquire before you make a decision?

Temptations

What is the potential for making a biased decision? In particular, how can you ensure you aren't making a decision based on an emotional response?

Options

What are your options? Take some time to think through other ideas, and don't just do the first thing you think of. What else could you do?

Plan

This could be as simple as a short to-do list or a more complex plan, depending what is involved.

Using STOP can help you be less impulsive and more rational. However, the model doesn't mean you should ignore *or* trust your intuition. Your gut feeling can often help you make difficult decisions as part of a properly considered process. We would argue that the very best decisions are taken based on a good slug of logic combined with a dash of intuition.

The very best decisions are taken based on a good slug of logic combined with a dash of intuition

Angela Merkel made her point when she said: 'Fear has never been a good advisor, neither in our personal lives nor in our society.' In times of crisis, Merkel does not shy away from making difficult decisions; during the Syrian refugee crisis she had the moral courage to allow refugees into Germany, despite the political costs of the decision. She also said: 'As a leader, you will be called upon to make tough decisions. Don't back away from them. Instead, be bold and take a stand based on the information you have about the situation, your personal values, as well as the organisation's values and the possible outcomes that can arise from your decision. Make the best choice you can and then make course corrections if necessary. Your team will respond well to your decisiveness and it will allow your organisation to move forward.'

Nudges

- What is your balance between system one and system two decision making?

- How well do you limit the potential for your decisions to be biased?

- Might the STOP model be a useful tool for you or a colleague?

- To what extent do you allow yourself to trust your instincts?

Paint irresistible pictures

Setting an example is not the main means of influencing others; it is the only means. The task of leadership is to create an alignment of strengths so strong that it makes the system's weaknesses irrelevant.

PETER DRUCKER

Peter Ferdinand Drucker was born 1909 in Vienna, Austria, but lived most of his life in the US after escaping the attention of Nazis. He is best known as a management consultant, educator and author, whose writings contributed to the philosophical and practical foundations of the modern business corporation.

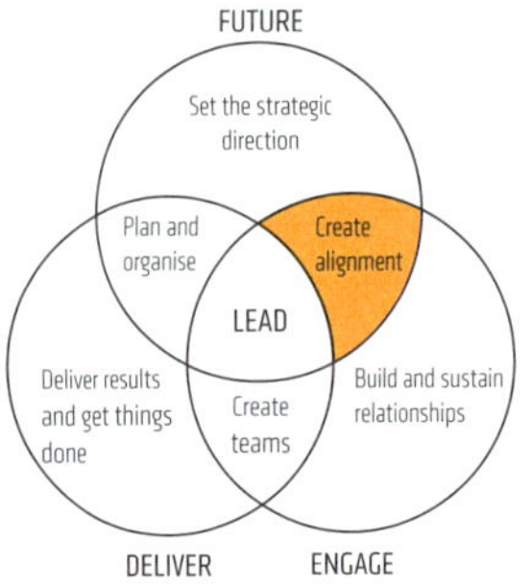

Leaders that paint an exciting picture of the future really help to build that shared sense of purpose. They create a strong alignment between the people and the vision, values and strategy of an organisation.

As we mentioned in Chapter 1, you can have a great group of staff that are really motivated and love their jobs, but if they aren't pulling together in pursuit of a set of shared goals and with a shared strategy, you won't achieve much. How you achieve a shared goal will, of course, depend on your context. But however you do it, having a clear set of strategies which underpin the culture you want to create and a group of people who have bought in to that approach, is at the heart of great delivery in any organisation or company.

There are several things you can do to create alignment within your team, and this chapter will examine some of those ideas. At the heart of alignment is great communication, which is of course about clarity of message but also about listening and observing carefully. Remember that communication is a two-way process; it's not just about what you say but, equally importantly, what you hear and observe.

Similarly, at the heart of creating clarity is great communication, whether that is in set-piece events or in everyday conversations. The best leaders continually reinforce their expectations and talk about them at every opportunity. They constantly show staff they value and appreciate the contribution an individual is making.

At the heart of creating clarity is great communication

On a day-to-day basis, when these leaders are doing a 'walk around' the workplace, they are looking for things to praise and comment on, both with management and staff. The odd passing comment can mean a great deal to the individuals concerned and maybe they have a better day as a result. This also reinforces to others what matters and what is important, the drip-feeding of expectations as part of everyday interactions can be very powerful.

Sometimes it is the quiet word to one side that is most effective, particularly if one knows the person doesn't like receiving praise publicly. For others, it is the public thanks at weekly briefings that is most important. Again, this not only motivates the individual concerned but also sends a message to other colleagues about what is important and valued.

The use of a personal note is probably one of the most effective ways of using praise to communicate and reinforce expectations

However, the most powerful way to praise is often through writing to colleagues. A handwritten note to someone, a copy to go on their personnel file, shows that a leader has taken the time and seen it as important to sit down and make a point of doing something personal. In terms of motivating staff and gaining their loyalty, the use of a personal note is probably one of the most effective ways of using praise to communicate and reinforce expectations.

There are several areas where clarity is particularly important and some of these are covered elsewhere in this book but the two that deserve further explanation within this chapter are the clarity of your outcomes and the clarity required for communication.

Clarity of outcomes

Clarity of purpose is particularly important and joining up the narrative is one of the most important jobs of a leader. Some of this relates to your mission and vision statements, but this is where we can dig a bit deeper. Clarity is about having defined outcomes and clear procedures. Good outcomes are the result of effective procedures being carried out well, and in any organisation procedural success is reliant on great communication which in turn is dependent upon interaction between mangers, staff and clients at all levels.

DEAN THOMAS

Dean Thomas says: 'As a business owner, a key driver for me was to devolve responsibility and not to micromanage. I believed that if the outcomes were clearly defined, with the right people I could achieve them. Tasks were allocated at the start of the month for completion by month end and assigned to individual team leaders.

Apart from the completion date, no further organisational instructions were given. This placed a great deal of responsibility on the team leader, someone key to the organisation and chosen for their ability to understand clearly the importance of the outcomes, and take total ownership and care for the business as if it were their own. Utilising internal and external resources, they were free to manage the work how they wanted. Although there was a lot of pressure and responsibility on the team leader, the autonomy and responsibility they were given made the role very rewarding. This worked well for the business and team leaders, evident by the fact they usually remained in place for many years. It reinforced my belief that if the expected outcomes are clear and you give the right person enough responsibility they will thrive and deliver.'

> ### The autonomy and responsibility they were given made the role very rewarding

He highlights the importance of freedom of operation within a clearly defined and communicated set of operational parameters and desired outcomes. Initial and ongoing training, and monitoring and evaluation are seen as essential components, as is the absolute clarity with which procedures – and the reasoning behind them – are communicated to staff and stakeholders.

It seems logical to follow established procedures but these often either don't exist or are not adhered to. Procedures take time to develop and embed, and your teams will need training to make sure they understand and follow them. If implemented correctly, good practices become a self-perpetuating part of your culture and will help your organisation continue to develop and move forward. Of course, armed with a long list of policies, there is always the danger that the workplace becomes overwhelmed by the sheer volume of rules and regulations; the very best operators get the balance just right. Creating a sense of shared purpose within an organisation is, as we have already mentioned, vital; every manager, employee and customer should be absolutely clear about what your business is trying to achieve and why.

Clarity of communication

The second area of focus is clarity of communication and having a consistent approach to communication at all levels of an organisation.

Communication is key to clarity

Dean Thomas explained: 'Communication is key to clarity, whether we were communicating with each other or our clients and this was instilled in every member of staff. In my company it was important that everyone could have access to everyone else. That meant if there was uncertainty or lack of clarity it could easily be resolved. If someone had the answer, no need to go through intermediaries, I encouraged them to go direct. Without a sales team, the building of long term relationships with clients was paramount. A lack of clarity in communication can lead to conflict because each party makes different assumptions about what is acceptable and what is not. This inevitably means that you need to develop a series of routines and procedures that cover all aspects of your workplace.'

Engaging others in creating the vision and strategy

Stephen Covey states that leaders, managers and employees at every level will need a holistic, integrated paradigm of what their organisation is all about, the dynamic environment in which it operates and an accurate understanding of how all the complex elements of their organisational ecosystem work together.

If you have the time, it's usually well worth designing a process that enables all interested parties to have a stake in helping to shape your vision and strategy. If people have had a say in determining the destination and how you might get there together, there is a much greater chance they will deliver their own part of the plan to a high standard when it comes to making things happen. This can be more relevant in certain areas than others, but even in busy departments where people are popping in and out every day, some operators are often left to their own devices for much of the time. In these circumstances, people need to be intrinsically motivated to do a great job as there is usually no one checking up on them.

Integrity

As Covey points out in *The Speed of Trust* (2006) it is important that leaders are honest, that they don't try to create false impressions or spin the truth. Not only does this build trust but it supports the creation of transparency and develops a culture where it is okay to talk about things that may not be working as well as they might. It is important in these situations to use simple language and describe things as they are and not to manipulate people or distort the facts.

There can sometimes be a temptation to work to hidden agendas or to keep certain facts or viewpoints from people, sometimes with their best interests at heart. In these situations, straight talking can often take courage.

There is clear evidence to suggest that organisations and companies which make the most progress don't allow issues to be swept under the carpet. They see problems that are openly talked about and shared with individuals and groups as opportunities for improvement. This creates honest dialogue and greater alignment. How such issues are raised however, is important, and care needs to be taken to pitch what is being said appropriately. Put too gently, and the point of what is being said may be lost. Put too bluntly, and any opportunity to change behaviour or move a situation forward may be missed.

Developing the skill to get this balance right is not easy and is another example of where leaders need to not only be self-aware but also attuned to the needs and situation of those with whom they are communicating. Making the space to step back and reflect in these circumstances is important, as too often the temptation is to rush into a conversation without really thinking about what sort of approach would be most effective.

Rob draws an example of this clear communication from his home life, he notes that one of the keys is allowing the whole family to be honest with each other. 'Right from an early age there was nothing we couldn't talk about, no taboo subjects. If a question got asked, it got answered; if feelings were expressed, they were talked through, we always tried to live in the now which was sometimes the long way around but often the most rewarding.' He suggests that these principles can contribute to your leadership style and that if you can be honest and consistent during the good times and the bad, you'll help inspire yourself and your team.

Influencing others

You are, like anyone in a leadership role, completely reliant upon other people to get the job done. For this reason, your ability to influence others is crucial. Not only do you need to be able to generate enthusiasm and excitement in the things you want your team to achieve together, you also need to be able to influence others outside the team who may have an indirect influence or impact on your work.

There are a number of reasons this matters. Depending on your role, you may, for example, want to implement a new marketing plan, introduce a new performance system for the whole organisation or establish a new code of conduct. Each of these will require buy-in from your staff. Of course, you can insist upon individuals implementing whatever you decide, but unless teams are convinced of the benefits of any change or new approach, you can be sure discretionary effort will be lower and the subsequent impact significantly reduced. Being able to appropriately influence members of your team will play a key role in ensuring changes are effectively introduced.

For middle managers, being able to influence externally is very important. Take, for example, decisions that others may take which have a direct effect on your team. You may wish to have some influence around decisions being made regarding whole organisation systems.

BEING ABLE TO APPROPRIATELY INFLUENCE MEMBERS OF YOUR TEAM WILL PLAY A KEY ROLE IN ENSURING CHANGES ARE EFFECTIVELY INTRODUCED

Or you may be keen to influence how new staff are inducted within your department. Or you may want a say around the detail of a marketing plan. In all these cases, decisions are being taken by others, often in the senior leadership team, that will have a direct effect on the work of your team. For this reason alone, it is important that you can exert influence when these decisions are taken. Yes, of course your line manager can act as your advocate if needed, but the more you are able to handle these discussions yourself, the better.

Most leaders are already very good at influencing others, having developed the skill very early in their careers, after all, it's precisely what they did day-in day-out to achieve a leadership role. But taking some time to think more systematically about how you influence others can be useful.

How you approach influencing someone needs to reflect the degree of influence you have

Degrees of influence

First of all, think though the different degrees of influence you may be able to exert. Those who you directly line manage are to some extent already under your control although, as already discussed, getting buy-in from others is still by far the most effective approach. Then there are those who you can have a direct influence on, but don't directly line manage. If you have a role in co-ordinating performance across an area, for example, you may well have a team of individuals where you are not the formal line manager. Then there are those where that influence may be indirect, where your ability to influence is dependent upon someone else. And there are those who you just need to accept you have no ability to influence whatsoever. Knowing this can save an awful lot of time and wasted energy. In a more senior role, while you have more hierarchical control in theory, it will usually only be indirectly through others that you can exert this influence.

IN A MORE SENIOR ROLE, WHILE YOU HAVE MORE HIERARCHICAL CONTROL IN THEORY, IT WILL USUALLY ONLY BE INDIRECTLY THROUGH OTHERS THAT YOU CAN EXERT THIS INFLUENCE

How you approach influencing someone needs to reflect the degree of influence you have. You can clearly afford to be far more assertive and directive with those who are under your control or over whom you have some direct influence. For those where you only have an indirect influence, you will usually need to adopt a subtler and less assertive approach.

Choosing how to influence

But there is another consideration. It can be helpful to think about the range of different ways in which you can influence others. Choosing the right approach will depend, once again, upon the context and the person you are trying to influence. Some situations are best handled with a straightforward and carefully thought through logical argument. In situations where the facts really do speak for themselves and the person you are seeking to influence is attracted to a logical argument, this is clearly going to be the best approach to adopt.

It can be helpful to think about the range of different ways in which you can influence others

This knowledge about the person you are seeking to influence is critical because for some people, the logic of an argument could be beaten, for example, by a more values-based pitch. Trying to use a logical argument with someone who is approaching an issue from a more emotional perspective is clearly not the best way of successfully influencing their view or decision. Paul Zak from the Peter Drucker Institute notes the importance of knowing your key people personally and says: 'When it comes to personal development, I inquire about family and home life. Personal life feeds back on professional performance and vice versa. We shouldn't pretend that it doesn't. There's also the issue of spirituality. Colleagues can interpret this dimension any way they like, but it assesses whether one is developing as a full human being. What are their outside-of-work passions? How are they making the planet and people around them better? Are they personally flourishing?'

You may also want to consider how much you're prepared to negotiate around an issue. This is particularly useful in situations where you have something that may be of value to those you seek to influence, for example you may have at your disposal financial resource, or you may be able to influence someone else for them. This 'you scratch my back, I'll scratch yours' approach can be a very powerful way of influencing some people. Of course, others may find it rather distasteful and be much more persuaded by an argument that appeals to their sense of moral purpose.

YOU MAY ALSO WANT TO CONSIDER HOW MUCH YOU'RE PREPARED TO NEGOTIATE AROUND AN ISSUE

Others can simply be persuaded by passion, energy and enthusiasm for a new idea. These are people who relish change, like to be in the thick of the action, and don't want to spend too long thinking through all the options.

Remember that people want to see you're not a corporate robot; it can be useful to show emotion in the form of compassion and empathy. But at the same time remember that learned behaviours will be more controlled than emotive ones; try not to react to emotive behaviours with emotion; react with logical, calm assertiveness. Professor Steve Peters describes these two parts of our brain as the 'human' part and the 'chimp' part in his revealing book *The Chimp Paradox*. He notes that both are useful but should be used appropriately. His model has been used by athletes, pilots and major businesses and can be applied to everyday life.

Try not to react to emotive behaviours with emotion

A skillful influencer, therefore, will be thinking about the extent of their influence, the context of the issue under discussion, and the likely response from the individuals they are trying to persuade. You probably already instinctively take these factors into consideration when persuading others but taking time to properly think through your approach is usually worthwhile. Identifying individuals who might be key to influencing others on your behalf is also very useful. As with all groups of people, there will usually be a few of your colleagues whom others tend to look up to or admire, or they might just be very vocal in the canteen. Either way, in certain circumstances, there is much to be gained by getting these opinion formers around to your way of thinking and allowing them to do your work for you in influencing others. Of course, this is often far from easy and may well not be appropriate or desirable in all situations. Entrepreneur John Gannon notes the importance of having an effective performance management process in place that all parties have agreed and subscribed to, as he says this is crucial in ensuring a worthwhile and manageable working relationship with those in your direct line, either above or below your current position, which is vital when it comes to exerting influence.

IDENTIFYING INDIVIDUALS WHO MIGHT BE KEY TO INFLUENCING OTHERS ON YOUR BEHALF IS ALSO VERY USEFUL

Continuing to try to influence people when they're not engaging can often be counter-productive

So, there is a lot you can do, but it's also important for you to know when to stop. Continuing to try to influence people when they're not engaging can often be counter-productive and cause others to dig their heels in. It can also mean that, on a future occasion, your ability to influence is diminished. It's a bit of a cliché but losing the battle to win the war can be a short-term price worth paying.

Nudges

- Do you take time to keep your messages simple and listen and observe carefully?

- Do you need to develop a clearer approach to outcomes?

- Do you have clear systems and procedures in place to manage communication and interaction effectively, thus creating a positive climate?

- Do you need to consider your approach to creating greater clarity in settings that extend to a group of companies?

- Would it help you to engage staff more with shaping vision and strategy, so you get greater buy-in?

- Think about the strategies and opportunities you have available to inspire others. Do you always make the most of them?

- What strategies do you use to influence others?

- Are these adjusted to the context or the person?

Lead up, across and down

ANNIE MCKEE

Annie McKee PhD is a best-selling author, executive coach and advisor to global leaders, from CEOs of Fortune Future 50 companies to government officials in South Africa. In 2005, Business Week named her in their list of Top 100 leaders.

Leading isn't just about working with your peers or those who happen to be more 'junior' than you. It's about being able to engage productively with everyone within your organisation and with your stakeholders. That includes your line manager and other senior colleagues. Building a strong shared understanding of one another's goals and challenges can be powerful.

When people talk about managing up, they often have some sense that it's about an individual trying to manipulate their boss in some way or even convince them to do something they otherwise wouldn't do. Managing up is therefore seen as somehow slightly dishonest or underhand, but actually, nothing could be further from the truth. Managing up, or as we prefer to call it, *leading up*, is all about making sure you have a productive relationship with your line manager that supports both of you to achieve the shared goals for the customers or stakeholders you both serve. It's about you taking your share of responsibility for the quality of your joint working relationship so you can both work towards mutually agreed goals that are in the best interests of you, your line manager and your organisation. It isn't political manoeuvring.

The benefits of leading up

If you are good at leading up, you can create a strong working relationship that benefits both yourself and your manager, so getting that relationship right is in everyone's interests. Like a great marriage though, it takes work from both parties.

For middle managers in particular, having a good relationship with your line manager can give you a direct route into the team above you. Not only can this lead to improved opportunities for you to gain experience beyond your current role, it is also a good way to help ensure members of your own team are on the radar of your senior colleagues. In other words, leading up is all about creating positive, mutually beneficial relationships for you, your team and the organisation as a whole.

Anita Roddick, founder of The Body Shop, worked tirelessly to stay connected and develop her relationships with her management team. She realised the importance of reaching everybody and was passionate about the company newsletter. She would suggest articles, check copy and change designs because she understood that the newsletter was a direct line of communication from the leader to the rest of the organisation. Roddick started life as an English and history teacher and knew that good, stimulating communication with every pupil was important; she carried this awareness into the business world, knowing that the channels of communication she had with each of her managers and staff members were equally important.

ANITA RODDICK

So, what does leading up actually involve?

There are a number of practical things you can do to strengthen relationships with your line manager. First of all, how aware are you of their expectations of you? Similarly, have you clearly articulated the expectations you have of them? For example, do you know how your line manager likes to receive information and how often? Do they prefer a regular e-mail update, or are they happy to let you get on with things on the basis that you will only get in touch if there's something you think they need to know?

In terms of your own needs, have you talked to them about the ways you like to work and the things you find energising? Do they know what can have a negative impact on your effectiveness at work? This is where using simple psychometric tools, such as those we offer at honk.org.uk, can be enormously useful. Beginning to articulate the things that motivate each of you can quickly lead to a more productive working relationship. As a line manager yourself, you may want to think about how you can enable these important conversations to happen with those you manage. Anita Roddick was almost obsessive about finding new ways to get across what she called 'that real sense of excitement.'

Don't just arrive at your manager's door with a problem

Secondly, when you are faced with an issue or concern, don't just arrive at your manager's door with a problem, but come with possible solutions and ideas about how it can be resolved. Roddick wholeheartedly agreed with empowering her employees and insisted on encouraging her line managers to think for themselves and make decisions; she said that empowering employees is the key to keeping them and that you empower them by creating a better training and education system.

Thirdly, if there are issues that are concerning you or if there are disagreements between you and them, it is usually beneficial for you both to try to address these sooner rather than later. It may well be the case that your line manager is blissfully unaware that you have a concern or worry. Getting these things out in the open as soon as they arise is beneficial to your relationship in the long run and enables the issues to be dealt with before they become an even bigger problem. John Gannon says: 'I have always been a big advocate of face-to-face communications rather than emails or text messages, particularly when there is a difficult, complicated or awkward problem that requires a resolution. In my experience an email exchange can often elongate the problem considerably and can indeed compound rather than resolve the problem. Put it this way: keep emailing = problem extension; talk it through = problem solving. The choice is simple. Pick up the phone or go and see the individual concerned face-to-face: it's a far more effective and efficient way of resolving difficulties.'

You should think about how you can give your line manager reassurance

It's important for you to be as honest as possible with your line manager; their trust in you can quickly be eroded if they discover you've tried to hide something from them or distort the truth. It's also important to remember that trust is more than just a measure of personal integrity, it's also about someone's view of a person's competence. This means you should think about how you can give your line manager reassurance that you know what you're doing and are delivering results. Taking opportunities to present well organised data and other information combined with good planning and personal efficiency will give them confidence that you're on top of the job.

John Gannon reminds us that an effective performance management process – of which managing up is part – requires the willingness of all. It's one thing to talk about performance management and entirely another to implement it and follow it up. Agree objective and subjective key performance indicators, and acknowledge that both parties need to adhere to, respect, understand and agree to take the whole process seriously, because if one of the parties feels it's a waste of time, it's bound to fail. Fergal spent an exorbitant amount of time in his company trying to get performance objectives exactly right and worked hard with directors to ensure they focused on this. Once you have a clear set of objectives which align with the organisation's goals and values, you have created a contract between line manager and direct report. The individual can then get on with the job in hand, knowing very clearly where they have to get to, even though they might need a bit of assistance to get them through the journey.

JOHN GANNON

When it comes to creating alignment, never underestimate the power of leading by example

When it comes to creating alignment, never underestimate the power of leading by example. If you can demonstrate through your own actions the success of a properly implemented idea, others will follow. It comes as a surprise to most leaders, whatever their role, just how much others notice the things they do and say. It is no good saying to others that it is important to always challenge staff about their poor communication with clients and then fail to articulate clearly as a leader. The old adage that it's not what you say but what you do that counts, sums up beautifully how this form of communication is crucial. One's behaviour can either powerfully reinforce expectations or quickly destroy them, which will either build or erode the trust and motivation of colleagues. It is critical to make sure you really do offer a strong example of what you wish others to do. To say one thing and do another can be extremely dispiriting and is likely to lead to poor implementation.

Anita Roddick's management principles were to lead by example by working hard and to see work as a labour of love, built on mutual respect between managers and employees and, ultimately, customers.

Great organisations are not islands

External partnerships

Great organisations are not islands, they see themselves as having a role which extends beyond their walls. This might include support for their immediate local community or other organisations in their field. Outreach work brings benefits to all concerned. Learning from outside one's own immediate context gives perspective and, often, new vision. But developing relationships with leaders in other areas isn't easy and takes time.

Regardless of your organisation's context, it's important to consider some key questions before entering into any type of organisational partnership or collaboration.

- What is the shared purpose for the partnership? What is the driver?
- What is the partnership aiming to achieve?

- What does the leadership of the partnership look like and where does it come from?

- What are the boundaries of the partnership and what is the governance?

- How does the partnership fit within the wider context of your organisation and other partnerships?

Within wider partnerships and your own team, if a key part of your role is to build and sustain relationships, there are inevitably times when you have to step in to manage conflict. While conflict is usually associated with negative consequences, it can also be a productive way to move a situation forward if handled carefully; constructive conflict where individuals are able to debate a point without it becoming personal, is an essential feature of high performing teams.

There are times when conflict can be debilitating

But there are times when conflict can be debilitating. It can arise in a whole range of different ways and with people from outside your team and within. It often arises because of resourcing issues, for example someone may have a disagreement with a colleague about how much funding a project needs or they may be unhappy about the limited progress of a department with – as they see it – a weaker manager at the helm. Conflict can also arise because of disagreements about who should be doing what. A lack of clarity on roles within your team can lead to people vying for position, particularly if they are manoeuvring themselves for promotion or other recognition. A classic example is when there are two people who are both organising the same thing, such as a presentation or a meeting agenda or an important whole-organisation initiative, where neither wants to cede ownership of the project. You also need to watch out that if things don't quite go to plan they can be quick to step back and look to point-score.

> A LACK OF CLARITY ON ROLES WITHIN YOUR TEAM CAN LEAD TO PEOPLE VYING FOR POSITION, PARTICULARLY IF THEY ARE MANOEUVRING THEMSELVES FOR PROMOTION OR OTHER RECOGNITION

Nudges

- Do you make the time to consciously manage your relationship with your line manager?

- Do you take your share of the responsibility for ensuring you understand one another's perspective?

- Is your relationship with your line manager characterised by honesty and trust?

- If it's not, what can you do about this?

- Can you see how a good relationship with your line manager can open lines of communication above and below you?

- To what extent do you engage with or enable productive partnerships with other organisations?

Help others to trust you more

MAHATMA GANDHI

Mahatma Gandhi was born in 1869, he practiced law in South Africa where he advocated for the civil rights of Indians, before returning to India where he became the primary leader of India's non-violent independence movement against British rule. He was murdered in 1948.

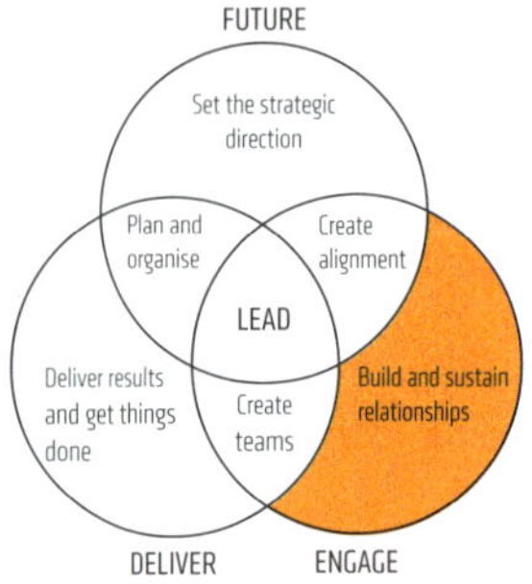

Building trust with the people you work with can have a powerful impact on how much you can achieve together. If people have trust in both your honesty and your abilities they will be far more likely to engage with you and what you want to achieve.

Building and sustaining relationships is one of the most important elements of any leader's role. As the popular quote attributed to Peter Drucker says: 'Culture eats strategy for breakfast'. The point is that you can have the greatest strategy in the world, but if relationships within the organisation, and between the organisation and its customers and stakeholders are not great, then outcomes will inevitably be poor.

Transparency matters

We know several organisations that have committed to 'confronting the brutal facts while never losing faith' (Jim Collins, 2001). Consequently, they have become completely transparent in the way they look at themselves, gather data, share and process information and draw conclusions about their next steps. They understand the need to establish the truth of a situation in their organisation in the strong belief that the right decisions will then become self-evident.

As one company puts it: 'If things are not working, we are encouraged to say so. This is underpinned by openness throughout the system, especially in terms of data and accountability. We work hard to keep things transparent, try not to use data or knowledge for blame but as a means to identify and tackle issues. This has not always been the case but is something that has evolved as our leaders have become more confident on the reliability of our data.'

If things are not working, we are encouraged to say so

Charity head, Amanda Tucker from Love my Hospital says: 'Without trust and transparency we have no legitimacy – if our donors, our clinical staff and our patients don't trust us and we are not transparent about how we manage what was ultimately someone else's money, there is in my opinion no charity.'

Using data and other information to monitor the performance of a team or individual staff members is a key part of any leader's role. However such a system is established, it needs to be understood by all employees at all levels and not just seen as an accountability tool for the senior team. Of course, accountability is important, there will always be the need for leaders at all levels to ensure their staff are performing well, and that solid evidence exists to make judgements about colleagues' effectiveness. However, for a team to become truly reflective, there has to be a strong professional trust centred on the information needed to bring about change for the better: better for your customers, better for your staff and better for your whole working environment.

For a team to become truly reflective, there has to be a strong professional trust

Keeping faith

Hopefully your data will tell a story of improvement over time, but this won't always be the case, and how you respond to worrying information is important. You might be tempted to bury bad news and carry on in the hope that things will get better – and sometimes they will – but if you don't grasp bad news and use it to learn and improve, an opportunity will be missed. To paraphrase Jim Collins, the best organisations will always confront the brutal facts but keep the faith that something can be done.

The best organisations will always confront the brutal facts but keep the faith that something can be done

USING DATA AND EVIDENCE TO SUPPORT THE DECISION MAKING PROCESS DEPERSONALISES THE ARGUMENTS AND USUALLY LEADS TO BETTER CHOICES BEING MADE

Creating a climate where transparency pervades all of a team's activity is not easy, but there are several practices you can adopt to support it. Firstly, you can ensure that when you are debating and discussing issues as a team, it is the merit of an argument, grounded in data and evidence, that is the basis for making decisions, not the force of a personality. Using data and evidence to support the decision making process depersonalises the arguments and usually leads to better choices being made.

Secondly, when things go wrong, examination of the underlying reasons needs to be conducted in a 'no-blame' way. This will be easier if you have created a climate where sensible experimentation and learning from mistakes is encouraged. What is needed is an approach of 'What went wrong and how can we work together to improve the situation?' rather than 'Whose bad idea was it to do that?' The focus should be on the facts alone, and what the team can learn from the experience. Mary Portas says: 'Honest face-to-face working relationships with colleagues are essential. I learned that you need open relationships where you're not scared to call it if something isn't working. The best business advice is candid and honest.'

Thirdly, you need to make sure there is an openness in the way decisions are made and communicated, preferably using an agreed set of principles that everyone can see are being fairly applied. Nothing is more divisive than colleagues thinking that a leader, at any level, has favourites or hidden agendas when it comes to allocating tasks and roles.

A charismatic leader can sometimes work against creating a culture of transparency

Responding to unwelcome news

Paradoxically, having a charismatic leader can sometimes work against creating a culture of transparency. A strong leader, who everyone wants to please, may be exactly the kind of person to whom it is difficult to bring bad news. Of course, how you as a leader respond to challenging information is important, if you give a defensive or irritated response, this will obviously tend to deter someone from raising issues again. It is equally unhelpful if you take no action to address their concerns. In either case, it is unlikely the person will bring up difficult issues again, which in the long run can be extremely damaging.

Highly successful teams operate in a climate and culture where information, data and decision making are shared openly and used supportively. These teams have 100% confidence in their own ability to bring about the changes required. In other words, they keep faith in their own capacity to overcome difficulties even in challenging circumstances. This resilience and inner strength come from a sense of common purpose and collaborative endeavour supported by strong and highly effective leadership that inspires the necessary confidence and self-belief.

It is important to create a climate of trust so you can concentrate your energies and talents on reaching your goals

The importance of trust

Collaboration and partnership are words commonly heard in large organisations and companies. While these are crucial elements of any success, too many decision makers talk about partnership working and co-operation without really considering the conditions that allow them to work. It is important to create a climate of trust so you can concentrate your energies and talents on reaching your goals, rather than on unproductive and misdirected activity or being suspicious about others' motives.

Jim Elliott, Deputy CEO at Norwich Clinical Commissioning Group reminds us that choices in healthcare are potentially very emotive and sensitive, and that difficult decisions have to be made in some very challenging areas. This is of course a factor in all industries, but as he points out; 'With the NHS this is very public, very political and can literally mean life or death for individuals with huge impact on wider families. Therefore by setting very clear priorities, supported

JIM ELLIOTT

by evidence, engaging and involving a wide range of stakeholders, particularly patients and by being very transparent and honest, trust and commitment can be developed. This is not easy, but experience suggests that a clear, honest and frank approach will be appreciated by people, both those receiving services and those delivering them.' This is real front-line management at its toughest, and he goes on to say: 'This is not the science of management, rather a human approach to recognising the impact of decisions taken in the abstract on individuals for whom the impact is real.'

In teams with a high level of trust, systems and procedures are helpfully aligned and bureaucracy is kept to a minimum

In his book *The Speed of Trust*, Stephen Covey (2008) sets out why building trust is so important for the success of any organisation. In his view, where levels of trust are low, staff will be working in an unproductive environment which is sometimes associated with unrest and often divided into political camps. It's an environment where bureaucracy slows down productivity and creates low levels of innovation and development. Inevitably, the discretionary effort that we explored in Chapter 2 is low.

In teams with a high level of trust, systems and procedures are helpfully aligned and bureaucracy is kept to a minimum. Individuals are trusted and supported to carry out their work. There are positive and transparent relationships among staff, leading to innovation, confidence and loyalty, and discretionary effort is high.

How do you build trust as a leader?

As Covey helpfully suggests, there are just two key elements to building people's trust in you.

People need to trust your character

Firstly, people need to trust your character. They need to know you have faith in them and care about their success as individuals. Finding ways, through the use of praise and feedback, to let people know when you think they are doing a great job, is the easiest way to do this. They also need to know they can trust your integrity. Do you respect others' confidences when they share personal or sensitive information? Do you avoid over-promising, so you can always do what you say you are going to do, even when this is difficult? Do you treat everyone fairly?

Demonstrate your competence and skill

When he left The Key, Fergal was told by many staff how buoyed up they had been by the hand-written cards received in recognition of good work they had done. Often the card would have been accompanied by a bar of posh chocolate. Indeed, staff would display such cards ostentatiously on their desks to celebrate their achievement and its recognition by the CEO.

Secondly, and often overlooked, they need to trust your competence and judgement. Your team need to be confident you know what you are doing, even if you don't always feel like you do. So, lead by example on things you are asking others to do. Demonstrate your competence and skill. This is a direct way of influencing others and helps create the culture of 'how we do things around here' as well as building confidence in your ability to deliver. I am not advocating you do this all the time, but it is a powerful way of building trust. The Key prized the power to write succinctly and clearly as primary skills, so Fergal would take time to write blog posts and notes to staff in as crisp a way as possible, in part to show them he knew exactly how to do what he was asking of them. Feedback suggested staff found this hugely helpful.

It is also important to make sure you regularly reflect on your strengths and weakness as a leader and work systematically and consistently on building those areas of strength as well as addressing those where you need to improve.

Overleaf is a useful summary of the key elements that Stephen Covey believes underpin a leader's ability to build trust.

THE KEY ELEMENTS OF TRUST
ADAPTED FROM STEPHEN COVEY'S *THE SPEED OF TRUST* (2008)

Exemplifying trust is an important symbol

Some of the examples that follow may appear somewhat simplistic, but they demonstrate – in a very straightforward way – where institutions have high levels of trust.

Teams with a high level of trust will *not* have systems and procedures designed primarily to check up on people. For example, if the head of a sales team requires their team to submit their sales figures to them daily, the team is likely to feel that the quality of their work and the level of their professionalism is in question. New entrants into your profession will need support, and peer-to-peer sharing of ideas is helpful, but trust is undermined where there is an implicit suggestion that someone cannot be trusted to complete work to an appropriate standard unless it is going to be checked.

Teams with a high level of trust will not have
systems and procedures designed primarily
to check up on people

A school, for example, where the locking of doors is deemed unnecessary by staff shows a high level of basic trust between all staff and pupils. Of course, there will be times when this trust is undermined by an individual, but a school with confidence in itself and its people sends a clear message to everyone. Not only that, but the time wasted when someone needs to enter a space that is locked and they don't have the key is a classic example of where a lack of trust can slow up proceedings and reduce productivity, motivation and effectiveness.

Another key indicator of a high trust organisation relates to processes for delegation, which are examined in more detail in Chapter 13. Clearly, good leaders will often delegate tasks, but to maintain high levels of trust, once something has been delegated, it is more empowering if the person concerned is left to carry it out. It can often be tempting to ask or advise a colleague about what is being done throughout the process, but this can create more work overall, make the person feel undervalued or not trusted, and is generally unproductive.

We learn more from the things we get wrong than the things we get right

In low risk situations, it is sometimes better to allow a colleague to fail and then review the process together afterwards. As Amanda Tucker says: 'We learn more from the things we get wrong than the things we get right.' The learning that can emerge is often far more powerful than if there had been an earlier intervention. Of course, if the person doesn't have the necessary skills or experience to cope with the task they have been given, then they are being set up to fail. Part of the skill of a good leader is knowing when to delegate and ensuring colleagues know they can ask for advice without any negative value judgement being made about their abilities.

Giving a group a small budget with which they can prioritise areas for spending can be very powerful

Trusting new team members

Showing your new recruits you trust them is very powerful. For example, encouraging your newcomers to consider issues that go beyond their job title will help build their confidence. Could they be trusted to input on financial decisions which will help them get a real grasp of what's important? Sometimes giving a group a small budget with which they can prioritise areas for spending can be very powerful. Or get teams involved in 'hack' days when they can work together on new ideas which they can present to senior management. What other leadership roles or areas of responsibility do you create for your staff? If you have a customer care issue, how much do you seek and trust the views of your new team members? Could they deal with it unaided?

New recruits are usually bright minds who are used to thinking, having just completed their education. Remember that they come to your place of work with a fresh set of eyes and can be surprisingly astute when it comes to making judgements about the quality of the deal they are getting or the quality of the deal you are offering to your customers or stakeholders.

The speed of trust

Finally, it is just worth considering how quickly trust can be built and how quickly it can be destroyed.

When it comes to people trusting competence, this can be established pretty quickly. In a modest way, you can discreetly make others aware of your track record. If you have been promoted internally this may not even be necessary. You can also ensure some quick wins which make everyone feel confident that you know what you are doing, and this injection of trust is usually slow to dissipate. People tend to cut you a bit of slack in the short term if something goes wrong, although you clearly need to make sure it doesn't become too regular an event.

Your integrity can be destroyed in an instant if you are found to have been dishonest about something

When it comes to your personal integrity however, precisely the opposite is true. It can take a while for people to know they can trust you to keep confidences, for example, or that you treat all your colleagues in a fair and equitable fashion. This needs testing before your colleagues will trust you; they need to know from experience. Conversely, your integrity can be destroyed in an instant if you are found to have been dishonest about something or betrayed a confidence. Be careful: if this happens it can mean some people will never trust you again.

Showing loyalty

We have already talked about the fact that all organisations and individuals can face challenges and difficult times. What good leaders appear to do in these circumstances is keep faith with the individuals that make the organisation successful. There is a clear link here with developing a 'no-blame' culture. Just because someone has made an error of judgement about a task or said something inappropriate to a client, doesn't mean leaders should suddenly forget the important contribution they make. In fact, quite the reverse is usually true. In these situations, what staff need to know is that they are supported and trusted and can be relied upon to learn from their mistakes and move forward.

The very best leaders give credit to all those who have enabled that success to happen

In contrast, when things are going well, the very best leaders give credit to all those who have enabled that success to happen. There is nothing more disheartening and likely to reduce trust than for an individual to see a leader take credit for something someone else did. Openly acknowledging the contribution of others is critical and shows real strength in a leader. This point is a fundamental passion of *Honk!*

Loyal leaders will speak up for an individual even when they may not be present and even if it may be uncomfortable to do so. Rest assured, word will get back and the person concerned will feel even more valued and motivated than they did before. This, in turn, builds momentum and alignment towards your collective goals. Loyal leaders also resist the temptation to 'bad-mouth' colleagues behind their backs. As mentioned previously, they respect the individual by dealing with them directly and raising any concerns face-to-face and in confidence.

So, to summarise, building trust has a significant impact on the culture and climate of any team. There are three key elements for you to keep in mind: showing faith in and care for the success of others; your own personal integrity; and your perceived competence and track record.

Nudges

- How open are you with data and other information?

- How good are you at confronting the brutal facts but keeping faith in your ability to overcome them?

- How could you find out about perceived levels of trust from your teams?

- If you identify there is a need to build trust, what are the actions you might take as a priority?

- Do you show respect for everyone you work with, regardless of their role?

- Are you loyal to colleagues, even when it is difficult to be so?

- Do you allow everybody to be recognised for their achievements?

Make people feel special

We sometimes underestimate the influence of the little things.

CHARLES W. CHESNUTT

An African-American essayist, author, and activist best known for his stories exploring race and social identity in the post-Civil War South. His work was revived in the 1960s for its relevance during the civil rights movement. A commemorative stamp of Charles W. Chesnutt was issued in 2008.

If leadership is about bringing out the best in people, then showing your colleagues you care about them can make a real difference to their motivation and, as a result, improve their effectiveness.

Stephen Covey (2008) is very clear about how the best leaders genuinely care for others and are naturally happy to show this in an open way. They respect the dignity of all staff members no matter what their role. Taking time to have a conversation with a cleaner who has a bad back is just as important as comforting a senior manager who has suffered a personal loss.

Leaders who take the time and trouble to do something to support a colleague, or who take a personal interest in a member of staff who is dealing with some tough problems at home, send a clear message to the whole workplace community that people matter to them. You can easily become so embroiled with your own problems on a day-to-day basis that you forget how important it is to get these things right. Jurgen Klopp, on arrival at the Melwood training ground as the new manager of Liverpool Football Club, called his first meeting and invited the whole staff, including the caterers, the grounds staff and the security guards as well as his first team squad; there were over 80 people present. He asked the players if they knew the first names of the staff, who were all doing their jobs to help them play football as well as possible. You can probably guess the answer but from that day forward he insisted they all learn and use each other's names every day.

Sending a card wishing someone well or arranging for some flowers to be sent takes a few minutes but can mean so much to the recipient. But more than this, it sends a message that colleagues matter as people and not just as employees, which buys loyalty and commitment. It reinforces the ethos throughout the organisation that your team and your staff are valued, and makes it a place people are proud to belong to and be a part of.

The cumulative effect of many small acts of kindness is immeasurable

The cumulative effect of many small acts of kindness is immeasurable. The little things that leaders do build morale and a sense of trust and play a significant role in developing momentum. If people feel valued and cared for, they reflect this by valuing and caring for the place they work and the people they work for. Jennifer Hodan, a former British Airways senior training instructor for cabin crew, says: 'At BA we talk about the importance of noticing people. How does it make you feel if you're noticed? How do you feel if you're not? Value contributions whether you agree with them or not. In a group discussion, you don't have to give your opinion necessarily; listen to a point of view and pick someone else out: "Do you agree?" "How does that differ in your role?" and they can perhaps correct, disagree, show the other side, even make someone else see the error of their ways without you needing to. As long as you keep the discussion on track you become the facilitator rather than the corporate voice.'

You can imagine the detail these people need to understand in their work. Jennifer continues: 'With all staff you need to notice them to motivate them. Manage underperformance, reward high performance, respond to feedback, encourage ownership and taking informed risks. All this depends on the individual and their strengths and weaknesses being noticed.'

If you model that type of behaviour to your staff, they in turn gain greater trust in you and a sense of belonging to their workplace. It is a very simple, virtuous cycle that leaders need to remind themselves of frequently, particularly during times of stress when it becomes far more likely that the importance of respect and dignity might be overlooked.

Many of the best businesses we have worked with also make important statements about how they value their staff more generally. For example, most of these companies provide free tea and coffee in the staff area at all times, even though budgets can be tight. Others might offer a discounted catering service for staff meals, a discounted gym

IF YOU MODEL THAT TYPE OF BEHAVIOUR TO YOUR STAFF, THEY IN TURN GAIN GREATER TRUST IN YOU AND A SENSE OF BELONGING TO THEIR WORKPLACE

membership or perhaps a shower area for those wishing to cycle to work. Such gestures are highly symbolic and represent powerful ways of creating a climate where people naturally begin to act in a self-disciplined way because they feel valued.

In one business, the senior team goes to great lengths to make sure employees are, in their words, cherished

In one business, the senior team goes to great lengths to make sure employees are, in their words, cherished. This doesn't look the same for everyone, so a personalised approach is devised for each member of staff which ensures they feel valued and nurtured. Part of this means that every exceptional deed is personally recognised by the CEO.

The same company also ensures that relaxation is valued. Monday breakfasts, Friday cakes, fruit bowls and chocolates delivered to offices, end of quarter celebrations, social events, prizes and celebrations for good work, great practice and team spirit are all part of the mix. The CEO even says to the staff: 'If you hear of anything that one of our competitors is doing that means that they care more, then tell us and we will do it!'

People will forget what you said, people will forget what you did, but people will never forget how you made them feel

Jennifer Hodan says: 'At BA our work environment of course is always similar but the situations that we have to deal with are incredibly varied, and therefore our flexibility, our manner, our credibility, our enthusiasm and how we make people feel creates the environment that surrounds us and that's important for my teams and our customers.' As Maya Angelou reminds us: 'People will forget what you said, people will forget what you did, but people will never forget how you made them feel.'

Keeping reflective and creating time to think

Having a reflective approach to the job and a willingness to listen to colleagues is critical. Remembering the importance of asking the right questions rather than being expected to know all the answers fits with this approach. Many leaders we coach find this a useful way to support the process of reflection. Setting aside quality time and being supported by someone with the right skills can often make a real difference in helping leaders think through complex challenges.

An appreciation of the importance of learning about the personalities of those we manage is also helpful. While it is important not to overplay this, it is useful to employ some flexibility around how you manage different individuals. For example, most places of work have members of staff who are natural followers of systems and procedures but sometimes find it hard to see the bigger picture. They can easily become obsessed with perhaps relatively unimportant details, even to the point of getting quite stressed.

There may also be individuals who are great at thinking outside of the box but have a much more laissez-faire approach to certain situations which can undermine and frustrate colleagues when they don't follow procedures properly. Both types of person require a response, but the nature of this should reflect what leaders have learned about the individuals concerned and their different personalities.

Jennifer Hodan explains: 'When training airline employees, it's a CAA regulation that we must train Crew Resource Management (CRM) to all flying crew. It's a fascinating subject to do with managing yourself, others and situations, your resources as crew, and dealing with everyday and emergency situations. It covers subjects such as situational awareness, decision making, teamwork, and leadership; pilots and cabin crew performance is assessed on these markers. These are fundamental skills for airline employees but are also useful life skills and have been adapted for other industries such as the NHS. You can see how the smaller details are so important especially in this potentially challenging environment where the unexpected can and does happen.'

In general terms, the important thing is that leaders don't stop reflecting or learning. You look after your own personal and professional development and make time to step back and see the bigger picture.

Your relationship with your board or senior stakeholders

Leaders often reduce their capacity to think in a strategic way because they don't give themselves time to think, reflect and grow as leaders. The best leaders we work with have understood this and don't feel guilty about making quality time to reflect. If you are a CEO or senior manager, investing time in building your relationship with your board or senior stakeholders or a non-executive director can be an effective way to step back and take a strategic view. Your relationship with these people can give you the opportunity to build an open, honest and trusting relationship which will allow for healthy debate, challenge and recognition, all of which will make you more effective. Apart from anything else, it helps reduce that sense that it's 'lonely at the top'.

We tend to underestimate the impact of our own day-to-day personal behaviours and organisational skills

Day-to-day behaviours

Our own experience and working with hundreds of leaders of organisations and businesses over the years has taught us that we tend to underestimate the impact of our own day-to-day personal behaviours and organisational skills. For example, there is nothing more frustrating for colleagues than leaders who:

- don't reply to a letter or e-mail within a day of it being sent

- regularly turn up late to meetings because they have been dealing with 'more important' matters

- leave colleagues out of the loop regarding a particular issue or event

- forget to do things they said they would do or even do something different from what had been previously agreed

- ask for feedback at the end of an event and then fail to act upon it or even acknowledge the feedback the next time the event is organised

- don't meet deadlines that all staff are expected to meet

- make (often poor) decisions 'on the hoof' because they have failed to plan effectively.

NOT ONLY DO BADLY ORGANISED LEADERS HAVE A DIRECT NEGATIVE IMPACT ON THE AREAS THEY ARE MANAGING, THEY ALSO HAVE AN IMPACT ON LEADERSHIP CAPACITY MORE WIDELY

Not only do badly organised leaders have a direct negative impact on the areas they are managing, they also have an impact on leadership capacity more widely. Their ability to inspire and motivate is diminished, they don't have the same level of credibility with colleagues and morale is inevitably lower. Staff start to feel disenchanted and question why they should go the extra mile when their line manager doesn't appear to value them. Of course, most of the time, nothing could be further from the truth. Most leaders do value their colleagues, it's just that the implicit messages caused by poor organisational skills might suggest their focus on personal performance needs to be improved.

When things go wrong, the best leaders are up front in saying so. They take responsibility for not having delivered and talk about what they need to do differently in the future. This openness helps to build trust and transparency.

WHEN THINGS GO WRONG, THE BEST LEADERS ARE UP FRONT IN SAYING SO

Not forgetting to have some fun

The workplace can often be a stressful place. Expectations seem to grow every year, and staff seem to work increasingly long hours in pursuit of their goals. In such circumstances, it can be easy to forget the importance of having fun.

For all leaders this principle can operate on two levels. Firstly, it can permeate all their everyday interactions. Clearly there are some leaders for whom this will be easier than others but cracking a joke or making a witty comment when appropriate is the bread and butter of some of the best leaders at all levels. However, this can't be about individuals trying to be something they're not, particularly in terms of forced or inappropriate humour. Keeping a frame of mind where one tries to raise a smile can be important in lifting spirits and making work a more fun place to be, but it needs to be genuine and heartfelt.

Secondly, it is important to plan for plenty of occasions where all staff can socialise together and enjoy themselves in a relaxed environment. It is a chance for you to show your staff and team that they are valued and respected, and is also a way to build relationships and give people an opportunity to have fun together. Of course, this applies to middle managers with departments as well as more senior managers for whole workplace events.

The dividend earned from investing resources in providing for some special occasions can be huge

The dividend earned from investing resources in providing for some special occasions can be huge. They help to build trust, momentum, a sense of well-being, and reflect an organisation that cares for its people, and by extension is capable of developing them.

Nudges

- Do you show staff you care about them through the little things you do?

- How regularly do you do this?

- Do you need to systematise this in any way?

- Do you make time to have some fun?

Share the lead

When team members trust each other and know that everyone can admit when they're wrong, then conflict becomes nothing more than the pursuit of truth or the best possible answer.

PATRICK LENCIONI

Patrick Lencioni is founder and president of The Table Group, a firm dedicated to providing organisations with ideas, products and services that improve teamwork, clarity and employee engagement. He is the author of 11 best-selling books with over five million copies sold and was named in *Fortune* magazine as one of the 'ten new gurus you should know'.

We can all achieve more when we work well with others. When teams work together, organisations fly. The role of the leader is to act as the orchestral conductor, bringing people in at the right times, playing to their strengths and creating something special.

As a leader you will probably be working with a diverse range of individuals. Some of your staff may be very experienced, extremely confident and need little support and guidance from you. These individuals have a huge amount to give to the team. Bringing out the best in your high performers is vital, particularly as the temptation is to focus on those who are less experienced, less confident and look to you for assistance.

Some of your staff may be aware of their own strengths and weaknesses, whereas others will lack that self-knowledge. Some team members may be facing significant external pressures in other aspects in their lives. Some may be highly ambitious individuals, while others may be content with their current role and have no plans to take the next career step.

Your role is to help support these disparate groups of individuals and shape them into high performing teams committed to a shared vision, in a way that brings out the best in each of them. What follows is a summary of some of the things that can help shape your actions.

When thinking about teams and teamwork, it's probably worth taking a moment to think about what we mean by a team. The best definition we have come across is from Katzenbach and Smith (2003):

'... a small group of people with complementary skills who are committed to a common purpose, performance goals and approach for which they are mutually accountable.'

It's a powerful set of ideas. For your own team, how true are the different elements within this definition?

'... A SMALL GROUP OF PEOPLE WITH COMPLEMENTARY SKILLS WHO ARE COMMITTED TO A COMMON PURPOSE, PERFORMANCE GOALS AND APPROACH FOR WHICH THEY ARE MUTUALLY ACCOUNTABLE.'

- Is it the right size?

- Do you have a good blend of skills, experience and expertise?

- Do you care about the same things – is your purpose the same?

- Separate from this, has everyone bought into the performance goals you are working towards? Does everyone know what they are?

- Do you have an agreed high level strategy that you all believe in?

- Do all members of the team hold one another to account, not just the leader?

Taking time out from the day-to-day pressures of your role to reflect upon how your team is working together as a unit can be very productive

How well does your team work together?

Taking time out from the day-to-day pressures of your role to reflect upon how your team is working together as a unit can be very productive.

Much has been written about how high performing teams develop. We all know this doesn't happen overnight and that most teams go through a series of stages before they are really effective. The most well-known model for describing team development was created by Bruce Tuckman (1965), and is summarised by his four stages of *forming*, *storming*, *norming* and *performing*. There is a simple logic to his analysis that resonates in any workplace context. We can all probably think of a team that never got beyond the internal politics and jockeying for position that characterises the storming phase of a team's development. The Dutch men's football team are famous for their talent yet infamous for the in-fighting that has scuppered their success at major tournaments. It is interesting to note that Tuckman suggests trust doesn't appear until the final stage of his model. He would argue that trust takes time to build and is the product of how the team has built relationships over time.

A more recent model developed by Patrick Lencioni (2002), suggests that for a team to develop, trust needs to be there at the very beginning. Without trust, he would argue, team members can't properly debate and argue without it becoming personal, which results in superficial discussion and challenge that leads to poor decision making and performance. As with Tuckman, this is also a pretty compelling analysis.

A team model for your organisation

So who is right? Well in a sense, they both are. If we combine the two, we have a model which starts at the beginning with the formation of a team and goes on to show how the team can, by using the trust that has built up, go on to enjoy powerful debate and a shared sense of buy-in into the team's goals as well as the programmes needed to achieve them. In other words, trust is somewhere along the journey, rather than at the start or the end.

A MODEL FOR TEAM DEVELOPMENT

Formation

Early days; getting to know each other; lots of saying the right thing; not rocking the boat; OK but superficial relationships.

Adjustment

Personal views are asserted; people vying for position; lots of assumptions about motives; misunderstanding and bad feeling not uncommon; difficult time for the leader to manage.

Trust

Trust between team members is developing; they are comfortable in exposing their worries, fears, vulnerabilities and weaknesses; they are honest with one another; people feel valued, supported and respected by others in the team.

Debate

Team members trust one another enough to be able to disagree and argue about decisions and issues without it being personal; the focus is on doing the right thing, discovering the truth, not winning an argument.

Buy-in

There is genuine buy-in and a strong sense of commitment from all team members when key decisions are taken, even if there has been earlier disagreement, because all ideas and views have been properly considered.

Performance

Team members, not just the leader, do not hesitate to hold one another to account for their behaviours and adherence to decisions and standards; there is a shared sense of ownership of the whole team's goals; the team is acting as a single unit and performing highly.

Having a framework can help a team reflect on how it works together. With the day-to-day pressures of any workplace, teams can be forgiven for sometimes not making time to review strategic goals and the progress being made towards them. It is even harder to devote valuable time to stepping back and reflecting on how well your team is actually functioning, yet doing so is critical. To be moving forward together effectively, a team needs to be working in a way that harnesses the strengths and talents of everyone in the team and challenges itself to be even better.

A team needs to be working in a way that harnesses the strengths and talents of everyone in the team and challenges itself to be even better

There need to be periodic checks of all the vital components and maybe the renewal of some of the basic elements to ensure smooth running. Using a model of team development can be one useful way of diagnosing how well your team is working. But finding time to actually use this analysis to improve methodology and re-charge team relationships is just as important.

Jim Elliott reflects on this in the context of healthcare: 'The NHS is primarily a staff based organisation, one of the biggest employers in the world, therefore being clear where individuals, teams, departments, directorates and organisations fit in the process is critical. The end point – a world class health service – is only deliverable by each of the component  parts functioning well and delivering their part of the process. Every individual has a key part to play. Setting out the overall NHS objectives, and ensuring that these are reflected in all objective ways forms the basis for an NHS "team". In essence the whole being greater than the sum of the parts, but the whole being totally dependent on the delivery of each of those parts.'

Developing leadership talent

Within the wider context of developing your staff, another key thing that great organisations, companies or sports teams are good at is identifying and nurturing talent. Whatever your current level of leadership you can probably spot future middle and senior leaders among those you work with. Apart from the obvious benefits for succession planning within your own team or group of teams, we all have a responsibility to develop the pipeline of the next generation of leaders across the country.

Great organisations have systematic programmes of leadership development in place to do just this. As well as opportunities for learning about leadership in theory, critical elements of these programmes include the chance to take on new roles and experiences, work-shadow and have coach or mentor support. We have worked within several groups of businesses to help them do just this across more than one area, which opens up a whole range of other exciting opportunities.

But there are some things we need to be better at in this regard. We still don't think we are good enough at recognising the inherent unconscious bias we all have, ourselves included, that tends to see 'potential' as looking like us. By recruiting and developing staff according to the norms that already exist, we run the risk that future leadership roles will continue to be dominated by white males, who some would argue, may tend to lead in a certain way. When we talk about knowing and understanding the strengths and talents of others in your team, it can help to remember that different leaders bring different strengths. Not everyone should conform to a certain view of what a leader looks like.

We also need to make it easier, for women in particular – but not exclusively – to combine the challenges and pressures of working as a leader with family life. Again, this requires CEOs and system leaders to think more creatively and differently about how they can be more flexible in the way things are organised within the workplace. The millennial generation is looking at new ways of working and we have to build this thought process into the reality of what we can offer them.

While addressing the crowd at the first ever White House Summit on Working Families, President Barrack Obama made a point to highlight the father's role in balancing work and family life. 'Too often, these issues are thought of as women's issues, which I guess means you can kind of scoot them aside a little bit,' he said. 'But anything that makes life harder for women makes life harder for families and makes life harder for children. This is about you too, men.' He encouraged men to start talking about how to better navigate the balance.

BARRACK OBAMA

Recruitment

Great teams, just like great companies, don't usually happen by accident. Care and attention are paid to each workplace recruitment process. Advertisements are attractive, the interview is thorough and professional, and organisations are not afraid to take the decision not to appoint and start over again if a suitable candidate fails to materialise. The more successful the organisation becomes, the easier it gets to recruit and the higher the bar can be set. Increasingly, great companies and their board members are using professional recruitment services, particularly for more senior appointments.

Patrick Lencioni, in his book *The Ideal Team Player: How to Recognise and Cultivate The Three Essential Virtues* lays out three traits that recruiters need to test for in order to hire team players; traits which, he argues, are more important than skills alone:

PATRICK LENCIONI

- Humble – does not think less of self, but thinks of self less.

- Hungry – aggressively pursues goals.

- Smart – emotionally smart, that is, in interactions with others.

At a Society for Human Resource Management (SHRM) conference, Lencioni argued that in order to hire team players, recruiters need to look for candidates who are humble, hungry and smart, and that candidates who have just one or two of those traits won't help your team succeed, and can sometimes even cause damage.

By the same token, you may need to be prepared to take a risk by overstaffing if the recruitment process produces two outstanding candidates for a post. Clearly financial constraints mean this is not possible in all circumstances, but in core areas particularly, there is evidence to show this approach pays dividends in the longer term.

When one of the primary schools Andy used to work with needed to appoint an assistant headteacher, the candidates that were finally shortlisted were each so good that the school appointed all three, despite the short-term impact on the budget. As a result, the school had three excellent class teachers as well as three highly effective senior leaders who worked together to help the school become outstanding. This can be an excellent tactic and not one we would all think to use.

New appointees need to fit with your organisation's, company's or team's core values

Thinking back to what builds discretionary effort, new appointees need to fit with your organisation's, company's or team's core values. The recruitment process needs to assess whether the person is aware of the vision and shares in the values that underpin your work and has a genuine passion for the job on offer. One business that we heard from asks potential candidates to read the company's mission and vision statements online and then asks questions at interview based on these documents. Such an approach not only tests their understanding of expectations but also says something about their self-motivation, organisational skills and how much they want to work for you.

IF YOU WANT TO DELEGATE TO OTHERS MORE, YOU NEED TO HAVE PEOPLE WHO CAN WORK WITHOUT BEING TIGHTLY MANAGED AND WHILE THEY MAY NEED TO BE GUIDED, LED AND TAUGHT, DO NOT REQUIRE CONSTANT SUPERVISION

If you want to delegate to others more, you need to have people who can work without being tightly managed and while they may need to be guided, led and taught, do not require constant supervision. Too much time can be spent on motivating and monitoring a colleague and then the situation rapidly becomes mutually unproductive. The right people will be largely self-motivating and self-disciplined, compulsively driven to do the best they can. Effective colleagues will also demonstrate a genuinely mature team approach to their work. For example, when things are going well they will identify those people who have contributed to that success, and when there has been a problem they will take responsibility rather than blame others.

The very best workplaces also take time to consider what balance is needed within any given team. One of the outstanding companies that Andy worked with uses the *StrengthsFinder* system when appointing staff. As well as the usual interview process as part of their recruitment, they ask prospective staff to undertake a *StrengthsFinder* questionnaire to better understand what individuals have to offer and how they will complement the needs of a particular team. They use this knowledge to ensure that employees are given roles which play to their strengths. Using this approach has also given the company a common language when discussing the strengths or weaknesses of its work.

USING THIS APPROACH HAS ALSO GIVEN THE COMPANY A COMMON LANGUAGE WHEN DISCUSSING THE STRENGTHS OR WEAKNESSES OF ITS WORK

Retention

Great teams need stability. To retain good employees, it is important to make sure achievements are recognised, working conditions are good, staff can see progression in their career and that staffing structures are flexible enough to allow this to happen. More generally, there is no substitute for ensuring everything comes together to make the ethos of the workplace as positive and energetic as possible; specifically, what leaders can do to build discretionary effort and a sense of engagement. People like to work in a place that feels good about itself.

People like to work in a place that feels good about itself

Indeed, such organisations tend to have a generally stable staff, running contrary to the common view that a good turnover is necessary to bring in new experience and provide opportunities for professional development. This lower staff turnover means it is easier for teams to maintain consistency in the way procedures and systems are followed. It also helps to foster strong relationships between the management and staff and between the organisation and its customers or stakeholders, as well as promoting a strong team-based approach to embedding a deep-rooted culture within the work place.

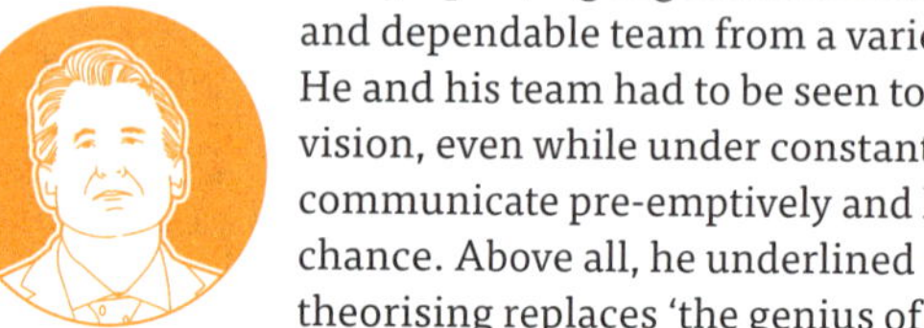

Sebastian Coe, when talking about the development team he created for the 2012 London Olympics, highlighted the need to build a resilient and dependable team from a variety of backgrounds. He and his team had to be seen to deliver on the vision, even while under constant scrutiny, and to communicate pre-emptively and leave nothing to chance. Above all, he underlined that no amount of theorising replaces 'the genius of hard work.'

A leader that Andy worked with believes staff turnover is low partly because of in-house professional development and the opportunities provided for staff to take on temporary responsibilities. The business has developed its own web-based 'me and my career' model for staff, which suggests activities and training at each stage in their career. Staff can complete the activities at their own pace and are then well placed for promotion.

Visit honk.org.uk to see our fully automated tool which allows members of any team in your place of work to gather views on how effectively that team is working. Most often used by senior teams, it asks a series of questions that are converted into a visual representation of the team's effectiveness. The tool is based on the team development model. New thinking on solutions can be created specifically for your organisation, you just need to allow some time to build something appropriate and then the time to make it happen.

Delegation

The job of any leader is never done. Your to-do list keeps getting longer. The scale of the pressures and expectations never seems to diminish. And of course, one can add to that the pressure you usually place on yourself to do everything to a high standard, on time, and in a way that makes the biggest difference for your team.

When done well, delegation is a virtuous circle where all parties feel engaged, trusted and have a decent work-life balance

The effective use of delegation will relieve some of the pressures you find yourself under, and empower, enable and support members of your team to take their next professional steps. When done well, delegation is a virtuous circle where all parties feel engaged, trusted and have a decent work-life balance.

Making delegation work

It isn't easy. When it comes to giving someone else in your team responsibility for writing a marketing plan, for example, or leading on a sales pitch, there's always that nagging doubt in the back of your mind that you could probably do the job quicker and better than the person you are thinking of delegating it to. On the other hand, failing to delegate effectively to members of your team can leave them feeling they're given insufficient responsibility or that when they are, your micromanagement leaves them feeling undervalued and distrusted. Amanda Tucker, head of the charity Love Your Hospital says: 'The team is everything, we all have our strengths and weaknesses and I believe that my role is to allow everyone the safe space to make mistakes. Sometimes it is important to give someone a task that will stretch them and is outside of their comfort zone, because only if people feel it is safe to make mistakes, will they achieve their best. We learn more from the things we get wrong than the things we get right.' This idea of giving people the space to get things wrong is important and can work well if your systems for following up and de-briefing are in place.

THE TEAM IS EVERYTHING, WE ALL HAVE OUR STRENGTHS AND WEAKNESSES AND I BELIEVE THAT MY ROLE IS TO ALLOW EVERYONE THE SAFE SPACE TO MAKE MISTAKES

Too much delegation can be seen as an abdication of responsibility

On the other hand, too much delegation can be seen as an abdication of responsibility, or as laziness or a lack of interest. This shows a lack of respect for the task at hand, and the people you pass it on to, so it's important to judge wisely, and make sure that when you delegate, others do not see the negatives, but instead feel empowered and trusted.

So what makes for effective delegation?

First of all, you need to consider what you're delegating and why you're delegating it. Be honest with yourself, are you delegating to develop your team, or just to get rid of work you don't like?

Secondly, to be a good delegator you need to be able to let go, you can't continue to control everything. If you are trying to do too much, you should hand over those tasks that are stopping you from reaching your full potential. The model from The Hay Group (2007) shows the three elements that need to be in place for successful delegation.

When thinking about delegating, remember that people can be most effective as leaders, and are most likely to take responsibility, when three things are in place:

- They have the *capability* they need, which includes skills and resources. Without this, they will feel vulnerable.

- They have the *authority* to act, to be an acknowledged decision maker in that field. Without this, they will feel frustrated.

- They are *accountable* for how they act. Without this, they could become complacent.

You need to ensure a task is suitable for delegation and can be successfully achieved by the person you're delegating to, anything else would be unfair and probably counterproductive. In addition, it's important to be clear about the task, its scope, and the expected outcomes. People like to have clarity about what's expected of them, so they can do a good job and not disappoint.

People like to have clarity about what's expected of them, so they can do a good job and not disappoint

Create a delegation plan

Some people find it helpful to use a matrix showing members of a team, the main things the team is trying to achieve and the skills and experience each individual is gaining. Through this transparent approach, you show the whole team that you are keen to enable a fair and even distribution of responsibilities and ensure that each of them has a chance to take on new challenges and develop professionally.

Linking delegation to performance development can also be very powerful. If in discussions with your team, you can identify a development area for each team member, you have a positive way in to delegating tasks that will help those individuals build the skills and experience they are seeking to develop. As discussed earlier, when it comes to motivating and influencing others, it's important for you to put yourself in the position of the other person and understand their internal motivations and personal drivers. If, when delegating, you're able to align what you need to have done with what people are looking to develop, you have created the classic win-win situation. That is why looking at delegation in the round and considering the needs of all your team when drawing up your delegation plan has such potential. Working in this way, you are able to create the best fit across the whole of your team.

At his company, Fergal's product director had very clear objectives for any particular period, as shown overleaf.

Build a best-in-class team of product managers whose decisions improve adoption, usage and retention term on term.		
Measurable key result	**Stretch/committed**	**Date of completion**
Design model approach to product management and evaluate skills across the team	Committed	30th Sept
Develop personal and team level development plans to raise performance, specifically data analysis, commercial leadership and user research	Committed	7th Sept: plans in place 28th Feb: average score >2.8 31st Aug: average score > 3.3
Individual strategies for each product in place, with one North Star metric each	Committed	1st Oct: final targets agreed post portfolio work
NPS scores for each product that increase quarter on quarter	Committed	31st Dec, 30th Apr, 31st Aug

DIRECTOR OBJECTIVES

Fergal expected his director to design his own work plan to achieve these objectives but would check in with him each week to get updates, to be available for support and challenge, and to offer perspective. For example, the objective around team development required a lot of trial and error and the weekly conversation would help them to reflect on this. He often received feedback from his direct reports that they appreciated the balance of trust and support that he gave them.

Gareth Southgate, the England football manager that Rob thinks has brought intelligence into the job, talks of the importance of 'independent thinkers' and wanting players to 'own the process' and take 'personal responsibility.' In an interview he said his deepest fear was not delegating power to his team but infantilising them. 'If you take responsibility away from players, they are likely to go missing when it really matters' he said. 'It may feel good as coach to have all the power, but it betrays the team.'

Consider providing coaching or mentoring support for members of your team

Also linked to developing the performance of your team is making sure that, together, you take time to identify any training needs. If you're asking one of the team to take a lead on data across the team or at a whole organisation level, then make sure they have, or are developing, the skills required. Consider providing coaching or mentoring support for members of your team. This could be from within the team, from elsewhere in the organisation or from an outside provider. It can be helpful to have the support and guidance of someone who is not part of the direct line management chain to help them get to grips with what they are facing.

A framework for delegation

When delegating tasks, be flexible about how the delegation will work in practice but remember to retain clarity around your expectations. Consider using a delegation framework to identify the precise degree to which you are delegating. For example, when taking a decision, does someone you're delegating to need to ask you for permission, ask for your advice and then decide or just tell you what they have done after the event?

DOES SOMEONE YOU'RE DELEGATING TO NEED TO ASK YOU FOR PERMISSION, ASK FOR YOUR ADVICE AND THEN DECIDE OR JUST TELL YOU WHAT THEY HAVE DONE AFTER THE EVENT?

There is a very simple framework that describes nine clear levels of delegation where level one represents no delegation whatsoever and level nine is, in effect, fully distributed leadership.

1. Look into this problem. Give me all the facts. I will decide what to do.

2. Let me know the alternatives available, with the pros and cons of each. I will decide what to select.

3. Let me know the criteria for your recommendation, which alternatives you have identified, and which one appears best to you, with any risk identified. I will make the decision.

4. Recommend a course of action for my approval.

5. Let me know what you intend to do. Delay action until I approve.

6. Let me know what you intend to do. Do it unless I say not to.

7. Take action. Let me know what you did. Let me know how it turns out.

8. Take action. Communicate with me only if your action is unsuccessful.

9. Take action. No further communication with me is necessary.

This framework can be a useful way of agreeing where on the continuum colleagues would like to operate. Of course, the further down the continuum one moves, the greater the degree of trust one needs to show in a team member, and the greater degree of confidence they need to have in themselves to complete the delegated task or role successfully.

If old-fashioned leadership was about exercising power, modern leadership is about judiciously delegating power

As part of a delegated task or role, it's important to reach agreement on the timeline, any deadlines, and an updating procedure. Once this has been done, it can be useful to ask the team member to write up briefly what they think has been delegated, how they will take decisions and when they will report back. This is a good way of both empowering them to own the task as well as giving you the opportunity to check they understand what has been agreed.

Across the social sciences, research is revealing the profound gains in productivity when professionals are handed more discretion over their work. The corresponding culture can boost confidence and motivation, and strengthen the bonds between team members. If old-fashioned leadership was about exercising power, modern leadership is about judiciously delegating power. This does not weaken the chain of command, it strengthens it.

IDENTIFY WHAT'S GONE WRONG, TRY TO UNDERSTAND TOGETHER HOW THIS HAS HAPPENED

Finally, it is important for you to let people know how they are doing and if they are achieving their goals. If there are problems, you should try to avoid going into blame mode. Rather, identify what's gone wrong, try to understand together how this has happened and, ideally in a coaching conversation, help the team member to work out what needs to be done differently. That way, they continue to feel trusted but at the same time can learn from their experience and improve on their work. It is your responsibility, as the team leader, to absorb the consequences of failure and create a culture where setbacks are an opportunity to learn and grow.

1. When you delegate, make sure the other person is set up to succeed because they have the capacity and competence (with support if needed) to achieve the task.

2. Make sure there is clarity about what is required, by when and to what standard. People usually don't know all the detail you have in your head.

3. Be patient. Remember that to start with it is unlikely that the person you are delegating to will carry out the task as well or as fast as you would.

4. Don't assume how much the person wants you to keep close to the task. Have a conversation. This will avoid them thinking you are either micromanaging or, at the other extreme, that you have abdicated your responsibility. Agree with them the frequency and nature of check-in points.

5. Don't underestimate what people are keen or able to take on. Usually people are pleased to be asked, especially if you are playing to people's strengths or stretching them.

6. Make sure the people you delegate to have the authority and resources to get the job done. And don't just delegate all the boring jobs or those you'd rather not do.

7. Make sure you plan ahead and give people plenty of time, rather than using delegation only when you are under pressure for time yourself.

8. Make sure you don't delegate high risk or critical projects unless you are 100% sure the person can deliver them. It isn't fair to put someone under that pressure.

9. When you delegate, think about who else can help or what the interdependencies of the work might be. Might it be something to delegate to a team rather than a person?

10. Make sure you say thanks for a job well done!

TOP TIPS FOR EFFECTIVE DELEGATION

And when success has been achieved, don't forget to properly credit whoever is responsible. However you do it, it's important you pass on the credit for success, rather than let others think you have been responsible. Nothing is more dispiriting for a team than to see its leader stoke their own ego and take credit for something they didn't do.

Nudges

- How well does your team match the Katzenbach and Smith definition given at the start of this chapter?

- Where are you on the team development model?

- What might be a useful focus to help you and colleagues become even more effective?

- How much attention do you give to developing talent, recruitment and retention? What more could you do?

- Are you creating the right environment for your team for modern living and lifestyles?

- How well do you delegate?

- What could you do to make your delegation more effective?

- Does the framework for delegation offer a useful way to help with this?

Run meetings that matter

PAULA ABDUL

Paula Abdul was born in 1962 in California. A dancer and cheerleader while in college, she continued as a dancer and choreographer and eventually worked for the Jackson 5 before becoming a pop star in her own right during the 80s. She then stayed out of the public eye until she joined the judges' panel of the immensely popular show *American Idol* from 2002 to 2010.

The time you spend with colleagues either individually or collectively is precious. It is your opportunity to share your vision, build engagement and plan for success. Great one-to-one or team meetings can really make a difference to what you can achieve.

Face-to-face time has the potential to support the effective working of a team or, if badly handled, to have the reverse effect. In thinking about meetings, it's also worth remembering that what happens before or after a meeting can sometimes be just as important as the things that happen in the meeting.

At *Honk!* we have developed some straightforward guidelines for meetings and suggest the following pathway to help you make the most of this important time with your colleagues.

You need to remember it isn't your job to lead each item

Before a meeting

First of all, make sure you have a clear process for setting an agenda, prioritising items and clarifying who will lead each item. You need to remember it isn't your job to lead each item. The more others take the lead, the more you will be working as a team rather than as a group of individuals doing what they are told. You should aim to make sure each agenda item has a time allocation. It helps to be clear in advance what the outcome required for each item is – for information, discussion, or decision? Ensure you allow sufficient time for people to read papers in advance of the meeting and try to predict which areas for discussion may need careful handling and think about whether any pre-discussions may be appropriate.

During a meeting

At the start of the meeting it can sometimes be helpful for the chair to review the agenda and reprioritise if there seems to be insufficient time to cover all the items. When doing this, they should make sure they think about those items that are important, not just those that appear urgent.

Try to make sure you have agreed who is going to record any actions from the meeting and who is keeping an eye on timings. Sometimes it makes sense for this to be someone other than the person chairing the meeting. Whoever is chairing the meeting should try to create a climate where everyone can contribute. Sometimes this may mean inviting individuals to contribute, particularly if they are less confident, in a way that won't cause undue embarrassment or resentment. But the golden rule is to make sure all your meetings finish on time. This will require the whole team to resist the temptation to go off on a tangent or go into too much operational detail.

TRY TO MAKE SURE YOU HAVE AGREED WHO IS GOING TO RECORD ANY ACTIONS FROM THE MEETING AND WHO IS KEEPING AN EYE ON TIMINGS

At the end of the meeting, if it is helpful, try to take time to review the key actions

When you feel the time is right, you may want to suggest rotating the chair for the next meeting, this is a powerful way of showing the whole team that they will have an important role to play as well as giving them the opportunity to develop new skills. At the end of the meeting, if it is helpful, try to take time to review the key actions. Where appropriate, you should agree to the date and time of the next meeting and make sure you finish by thanking all the participants and finish on a positive note, however difficult earlier discussions may have been.

1. Be clear what type of meeting it is — what is it for?

2. Make sure the environment is right; offer refreshments.

3. Don't have a meeting for the sake of it.

4. Make sure the right people are there; use sub-groups.

5. Ensure there is plenty of notice of meetings and pre-work.

6. Have a clear agenda (prioritised; realistic; timed; owned).

7. Agree meeting protocols for discussion and stick to them.

8. Usually best not to *present* anything — send out pre-reading (in good time) and assume it has been read properly.

9. Keep a clear record of agreed actions.

10. Chair should: encourage participation; keep focus; keep to time.

11. Mobile technology protocols are clear and followed.

12. Rotate roles of chair and note-taker, where appropriate.

13. Clarify outcomes at the end and thank everyone.

14. Share notes of meeting promptly, with actions, owners and timelines.

15. Use pre- and post-meeting discussions to *oil the wheels*.

16. Participants should listen, respect others' views, be honest, challenge constructively, respect confidentiality and adhere to cabinet responsibility.

TOP TIPS FOR EFFECTIVE MEETINGS

After a meeting

Stress the importance of the note of actions being agreed and circulated promptly. Where there have been particularly sensitive discussions, consider whether a short post-discussion conversation may be appropriate with individuals. From time to time, ask people in the team for feedback. What can you do to improve your meetings?

Meeting protocols

Taking some of these ideas a stage further, one strategy we have seen used successfully in a number of organisations is that of developing a meeting protocol for how meetings are conducted. The outline below gives an example of how one of these works in practice.

Before the meeting

(1) Have a mechanism to agree two or three priority items.

(2) Circulate a short document that summarises

- who is the owner of the issue

- why it is important

- what the owner wants help with (such as advice for reflection or a decision to be made in the meeting)

- relevant pre-reading as background.

At the meeting

(1) Brief introduction by the owner of the issue.

(2) Each person, in order, gives the help asked for.

(3) Go round again.

(4) Final chance for a chip in.

(5) Owner summarises what they are taking away/makes decision.

USING A MEETING PROTOCOL

Getting your meeting structure right

For all leaders, particularly those in senior or system leadership roles, one of the challenges can be creating time for strategic discussion. In *The Advantage*, management guru Patrick Lencioni (2012) advocates thinking about meetings as being of three distinct types. We have shown below how his approach has been modified by one organisation to suit their particular context.

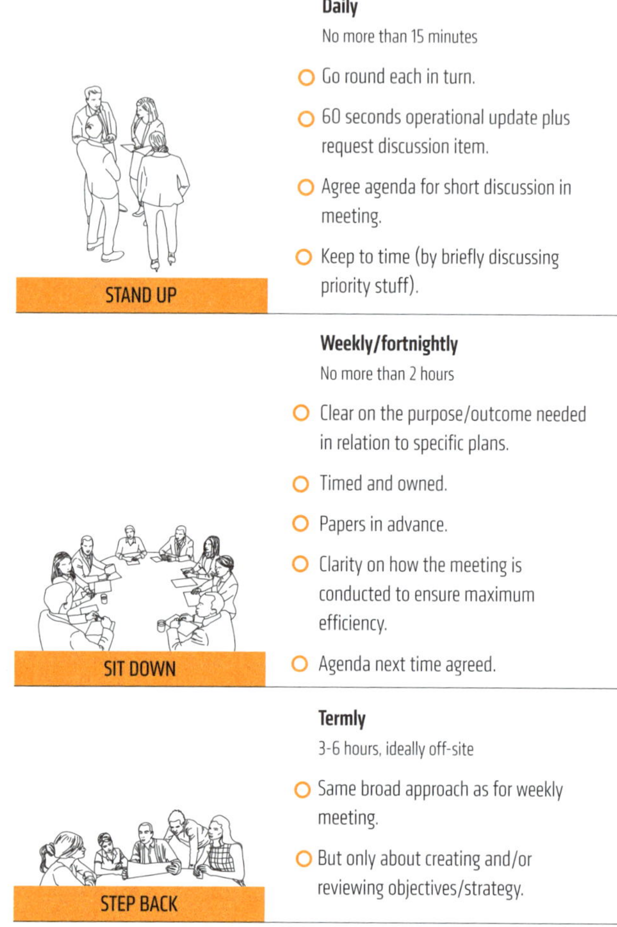

Daily

No more than 15 minutes

O Go round each in turn.

O 60 seconds operational update plus request discussion item.

O Agree agenda for short discussion in meeting.

O Keep to time (by briefly discussing priority stuff).

Weekly/fortnightly

No more than 2 hours

O Clear on the purpose/outcome needed in relation to specific plans.

O Timed and owned.

O Papers in advance.

O Clarity on how the meeting is conducted to ensure maximum efficiency.

O Agenda next time agreed.

Termly

3-6 hours, ideally off-site

O Same broad approach as for weekly meeting.

O But only about creating and/or reviewing objectives/strategy.

THREE TYPES OF MEETING
ADAPTED FROM A MODEL BY
LENCIONI IN *THE ADVANTAGE*
(2012)

1:1 meetings

While team meetings are obviously a powerful way to shape strategy and build engagement within a team, so too are 1:1 meetings.

Sitting down 1:1 with someone can be powerful. Of course, more formal appraisal and performance management processes are an important element of line management, but the power of the regular, developmental conversation is, in our view, at the heart of what really drives improvement and performance. Taking the time to agree how these conversations will work in practice is in itself an important part of the process.

These are some of the features of great 1:1 meetings:

1. Agree or contract with one another at the start how your 1:1s will work.

2. Schedule your 1:1s well in advance and avoid cancelling.

3. As you delegate more, let your team members each create their own agenda (maybe provide an agenda template to help) — add in your items afterwards. Decide if you will settle the agenda before or in the meeting.

4. Avoid the temptation for them to be updates — this can often be done in other ways. Try to make your 1:1s about things that need discussion.

5. Ask questions more than give advice. Make your 1:1s developmental.

6. Occasionally, ask for help with something you are working on that you would value their opinion or help with.

7. Make your 1:1s feel personal. Ask them how you can do this.

8. Try to ensure they leave feeling valued, energised and positive.

9. If you have any follow-up actions, try to do them the same day if you can.

10. Occasionally, ask for feedback on your own performance.

TOP TIPS FOR GREAT 1:1 MEETINGS

The key here is to avoid 1:1s being meetings where someone shows up and is just expected to account for themselves and their work. No one looks forward to meetings like this. While this is obviously sometimes necessary, finding other ways to do this can allow colleagues to bring ideas and discussion points to the table feeling empowered and trusted. During his work in education Andy states that he often used a quick pro-forma that he sent to his line manager in advance of the meeting to give an update on all the key areas of interest, so they both knew how tasks were progressing and could then focus on what they really needed to discuss together.

Avoid 1:1s being meetings where someone shows up and is just expected to account for themselves and their work

Meetings should be part of your team building process and points raised with individuals are of course part of the bigger picture and should be included in your team processes. John Gannon adds: '1:1 meetings are one element and play their part in team building and creating teams – you need to get to know your people to build effective teams and these are created by a range of features including effective performance management, reward, and an effective appraisal process, stimulating work environment, career progression, opportunity and challenge and a myriad of other elements.'

You may also find it useful for your team to use a personality tool, such as *Persona*, to help them understand one another's personalities. This doesn't just help you better understand your team, it also gives team members a better understanding of you. Some people find the use of these sorts of tools quite threatening, so taking time to talk through how best to introduce such an idea can be helpful.

PERSONA

Appraisal meetings

Although appraisal meetings can be relatively rare events, they simply shouldn't be. No matter how small or large your business or organisation, it is worth just taking a moment to think about appraisal or performance management meetings and where they fit into the bigger picture of an individual's development. For many smaller companies (and we've all been guilty of this) appraisals run the risk of being a one-off event around the beginning or end of a year and usually involve a discussion about money, but you'll find the two – appraising performance and setting financial reward – are best kept apart.

Lissie Whitaker, Director of Human Resources at the University of Chichester, says: 'Effective feedback helps us to become more aware of what we do and how we do it; receiving constructive feedback provides an opportunity to change and modify our actions in order to become more effective. Whatever the processes involved, appraisals should not become a substitute for on-going dialogue and feedback between managers and staff, but they are an important part nonetheless. Encouraging a culture that supports and encourages knowledge transfer, coaching, mentoring and employee development will support both individual and organisational effectiveness.'

To be really effective formal appraisal meetings should be properly aligned with more regular developmental 1:1s

1. Agree time and place well in advance, stick to these arrangements, and be well prepared for the meeting.

2. Give the appraisee time to reflect on their goals and rate themselves in advance.

3. Ask them to also think about areas for development ahead of the meeting.

4. Whenever possible, give some positive feedback at the start.

5. Make sure you have good evidence, collected from a range of sources which has ideally been shared in advance.

6. There should be no surprises. If there are performance concerns, they should be always be raised at the time they arise and support offered.

7. They should do more of the talking. Ask good questions to help them reflect for themselves on their strengths and areas for development.

8. Keep the meeting appropriately formal. It's not a social occasion and will usually matter a lot to the person being appraised. Take it seriously.

9. Take care in your write-up not to over-praise or miss out concerns. Both of these could come back to haunt you if performance dips.

10. Make sure new goals are SMART (specific, measurable, achievable, relevant and time-bound). Avoid setting goals that you both know will never be achieved.

11. Make sure you keep good notes and ask them to sign off (and comment, if they wish) on the final record of the meeting.

12. Ask for feedback on how you conducted the appraisal.

TOP TIPS FOR APPRAISAL MEETINGS

It has become increasingly evident to us that to be really effective formal appraisal meetings should be properly aligned with more regular developmental 1:1s that have a coaching focus.

At The Key, Fergal received 360 degree feedback on his direct reports from six people chosen by them, at least 48 hours in advance of the meeting. This was accompanied by the individual's own analysis of how they had done against each of their objectives and what they thought they needed to focus on in the next period. Fergal would typically spend one to two hours making notes from the feedback and shaping the points he wanted to make. The session would be led by the direct report rather than Fergal, although Fergal would always start by thanking the person and saying how they had contributed to the organisation's journey over the past period. The direct report would then talk through their objectives and how they had fared in relation to each one, what issues they had encountered, how the landscape had changed over the period and what they had learned.

It was typically a hugely developmental and useful 90-minute session for both parties and Fergal always asked for feedback as to how he could better support the individual. The company had spent huge amounts of time trying to improve the system and ended up investing in a digital platform called 'Small Improvements' that made the whole enterprise much easier to manage. Without a doubt, the appraisal system was one of the most impactful drivers of the company's success over the years.

Nudges

- How well do your meetings operate?

- How do you know?

- Is the structure of your meetings effective?

- Could the stand-up, sit-down, step-back model offer anything useful in your context?

- Have you talked with your team about what they would find useful when they are in a 1:1 with you?

- What about your line manager? Do they know what would work well for you?

- How well do you make time for discussion while making sure that all the basics are being done well?

- Might using a 1:1 update pro-forma be a useful way to help with this?

- How effective are your own appraisal meetings?

Don't drop the ball

However beautiful the strategy, you should occasionally look at the results.

WINSTON CHURCHILL

Sir Winston Churchill was a politician and military leader. Twice named prime minister of the United Kingdom, he forged alliances with the United States and Soviet Union to defeat Nazi Germany in World War 2.

JESSICA ENNIS

Your personal organisation can make a big difference to your own effectiveness as a leader as well as the levels of motivation or discretionary effort of those you work with. Get this right and the culture and climate within your team or organisation will significantly improve. Drop the ball, and others can lose confidence in you and become demotivated.

Olympic Heptathlon champion Jessica Ennis explains that to get to the top she had to be extremely organised, after all she had to master not just one but seven athletic events and even wrote her dissertation at university on 'self-regulation/ discipline'. In a YouTube video her mother said that for a time she thought Jessica was selfish because her training – a strict, six-day-a-week schedule – and her needs took priority over everything else. In response to this Jessica admits that she thinks her mum is right.

She says she does have to be quite a selfish person because of what she does. She simply has to be. It's an individual sport and so you have to be constantly looking at what's best for you, and everything has to fit in with where you want to get to. She thinks that changes through life, but when you're in the thick of it, you do have to be like that. Interestingly, she goes on to say that she doesn't want to think of life after competing, but if she were to do anything else she'd go down the psychology route as that's what interests her.

In Chapter 12 we examined the importance of those day-to-day actions where we can sometimes slip up. As a recap, here are some of the key things we identified which people find frustrating, such as leaders who:

- don't reply to a letter or e-mail within a day or two of it being sent

- regularly turn up late to meetings because they have been dealing with 'more important' matters

- leave colleagues out of the loop regarding a particular issue or event

- forget to do things they said they would do or more annoyingly they even do something different from what had been previously agreed

- ask for feedback at the end of an event and then fail to act upon it or even acknowledge the feedback the next time the event is organised

- don't meet deadlines that all employees are expected to meet

- make (often poor) decisions 'on the hoof' because they have failed to plan ahead effectively.

Keeping commitments

One of the most frustrating things for team members in any organisation is when someone senior doesn't keep a promise they made. It is probably the quickest way that trust can be destroyed. Yet honouring commitments, especially when it is clearly difficult to do so, is one of the most effective ways you can build confidence and trust with managers, staff and of course customers or stakeholders.

One of the most frustrating things for team members in any organisation is when someone senior doesn't keep a promise they made

Leaders can be tempted to wriggle out of commitments, often this will arise in situations where a promise is given before thinking through all its implications. For example, a senior manager who agrees, as a result of some special pleading, that a member of staff may have a reduced working day, may well find themselves in the position where other staff complain this is unfair. The temptation, of course, is to renege on the promise, yet it is probably wiser to honour the original agreement, openly acknowledge that a mistake has been made and apologise to other colleagues. It is the acknowledgement and apology which are critical here, trying to make excuses and blame changing circumstances can be tempting but reduces trust. Think commitments and promises through carefully before making them.

Personal organisation

Dean Thomas, entrepreneur and former business owner, told the following story:

'A key part of being organised for me was to be at work. I avoided the three-day week and time playing golf. This not only set an example but enabled me to be available and well organised.

The engine of the company was the team of administration staff. They were tightly organised into specific roles that followed set procedures and timeframes. Client facing staff had more freedom to organise themselves and were provided with the tools to help them do it. These would include smartphones, shared calendars and remote connectivity. They also received regular individualised reports from the admin system to tell them at what stage they were in a process in terms of work completed and work outstanding. This information was used to reorganise schedules and adjust priorities accordingly.

Although the company was run as a tight ship, I always tried to maintain a buffer in the system to accommodate unplanned work. To help with absence and holiday time, all staff had their core roles and one or two supplementary roles. A supplementary role was the core role of another staff member which they could step into and cover when needed. This was documented and regular meetings held to check status and effectiveness.

If the phone went, I automatically picked up my A4 pad

On a personal level, I wrote everything down. If the phone went, I automatically picked up my A4 pad, made an entry with a date and to whom I was speaking. I did this for clients and staff. For any task, I would note what was required and when it needed to be done by. For clients, I would reconfirm their requirements back via email so there would be no misunderstanding. To provide closure and provide a good service, I would email the client details when the request was completed. On numerous occasions I had to refer back to notes taken years previously. The day I sold the company I disposed of over 20 years of dated notes. I encouraged staff to adopt a similar approach and ensure that they were seen taking notes, as that always gave others confidence they were organised.

Everyone has what I call a 'too hard pile' on their desk. An ever-growing pile of paper or things that you are going to deal with later. I found that people were at their most organised just prior to going on holiday. All emails and correspondence dealt with and desk clear. I encouraged this 'going on holiday desk' and a tidy inbox at all times. Only outstanding items should be in the inbox, but at the same time never deleting emails. All dealt-with emails were archived to a Completed Mail folder which was easily accessed if needed. The state of an individual's desk and email system was a good indication of how organised they were.'

A surprising number of business leaders are not that predisposed to being well organised

Keeping on top of things

What systems do you have in place to make sure things you have decided, agreed or promised to do, get done? For some leaders, tight organisation might be a natural habit, for others it might be all about lists. But a surprising number of business leaders are not that predisposed to being well organised. The great news is, there are a number of simple and effective ways you can keep organised. One way is to use your email account to help. Many senior leaders Andy has worked with over the last few years have found this technique has really helped them. Here's how this system, which Andy still uses to this day, actually works, in his words:

Stage one: a job arrives

A particular task may arrive through different routes. Some may arise from a meeting, a conversation in the corridor or an email. Others may be things you decide for yourself you want to do. However your jobs arrive, what I find useful is having just one place where you store them.

Stage two: creating one place for your job list

For those tasks that don't arrive by email, you should ideally have one place (a notebook or diary) where jobs are written down. It may sound like a small point but bear with me because this next strategy really works. Next to your notes, where there is a task, draw a large circle. This serves to indicate that action is needed and will really stand out on the page.

When it comes to reviewing the empty circles – something you should ideally do at least once a day – you have two options: either do the job straight away and tick the circle, or send yourself an email with the task written in the email header.

This means you then have all your outstanding tasks in your email system. Given that many tasks arrive by email these days, this stage is often unnecessary, which is why this is so efficient as a methodology for managing jobs.

Stage three: managing your email

There is nothing worse for anybody than an overflowing inbox. It adds to that sense of feeling overloaded and overwhelmed. Andy has worked with leaders at all levels in the last few years and some of them have literally thousands of emails in their inbox. There has to be a better way.

There is nothing worse for anybody than an overflowing inbox

My suggestion is this: create just three email folders labelled Now, Soon and Later. You can then place emails into the appropriate box, (not forgetting the option to press delete) thus keeping your inbox clear.

You may of course want to vary how many folders you have or what you call them. You may also want to create other folders to archive emails you might want to find later, although I would suggest this isn't a great use of time. Much better to just store any email you think you may need again in your system's archive folder and use the search engine within your email account on the rare occasion you need to retrieve a particular message.

THE ADVANTAGE OF THIS SYSTEM IS THAT ALL YOUR JOBS ARE NOW IN ONE PLACE. RE-PRIORITISING IS EASY, YOU JUST MOVE EMAILS BETWEEN THE FOLDERS

The advantage of this system is that all your jobs are now in one place. Re-prioritising is easy, you just move emails between the folders. Schedule a short amount of time each day to review your *Now* and *Soon* boxes. You only need to review the *Later* box once a week to see if anything can be deleted (many can) or moved to *Now* or Soon because the time has come to action them.

This method has other benefits. When you are in a meeting or talking in a corridor and you have agreed to help out with something, why not just ask the other person to email you as a reminder. That serves two purposes: it means they have to make the effort to do this which means they really need your help, and you automatically have it in your tasks system, rather than having to transfer it from your notebook or that scrap of paper you wrote it on and lost, assuming you wrote something down at all. Many senior leaders in organisations and companies or business owners we work with think they are great at remembering to do things. They usually aren't – there are just too many things on that mental 'to do' list.

Using this simple email-based prioritisation system has transformed many leaders' personal effectiveness and their ability to prioritise efficiently. You may not need something like this, but if you are struggling with the sheer volume of tasks and worry that you may be dropping balls without even realising, it might be worth giving it a try

The commonly used analogy of the airline pilot is also useful here when discussing consistent delivery. Our expectation as a passenger on a plane is that 100% of the journeys undertaken will be successful, with a safe take-off, flight and landing every single time. It is no good to us as passengers if the pilot's performance is only 95%, they need to get it right every single time. It's that reliability that needs to start with us as leaders.

It is no good to us as passengers if the pilot's performance is only 95%, they need to get it right every single time

Building momentum

Of course, great delivery takes time to develop. In *Good to Great*, Jim Collins describes what he calls the 'flywheel concept'. He asks the reader to consider how a typical flywheel works. Its principal aim is to store energy and build momentum. Pushing a heavy cast-iron disc is incredibly difficult in the early stages and progress appears slow. Gradually, over time, with a concerted and sustained effort the flywheel will build its momentum. As more and more people join in pushing the flywheel so its speed will grow and grow until eventually everyone could let go and the flywheel would continue unimpeded.

People instinctively want to join something that is building and growing

The analogy works for organisations of any size. People instinctively want to join something that is building and growing. The fact that the departure of a key leader or other individuals does not mean the flywheel stops also effectively illustrates the importance of a whole organisation developing its own momentum rather than the alternative approach where the success of a place is dependent upon a single person or small group of people.

Reflecting on the leadership model that underpins this book, the flywheel analogy also reinforces the importance of alignment. If some people were pushing the flywheel in the opposite direction it would clearly not gain momentum. Everyone needs to be pushing in the same direction if success is to be achieved.

THIS IDEA OF GRADUALLY BUILDING PERFORMANCE AND DELIVERY OVER TIME, WITH A FOCUS ON INCREMENTAL IMPROVEMENT, UNDERPINS THE CONCEPT OF BUILDING MARGINAL GAINS

This idea of gradually building performance and delivery over time, with a focus on incremental improvement, underpins the concept of building marginal gains. This approach is exemplified by the success of the British cycling team which has concentrated on executing small changes really well. The combined impact of these changes has made them world class, with the team believing it is easier to make ten 1% improvements than one 10% change.

Momentum brings resilience and strength in depth

There are times when organisations encounter difficulties, and in these circumstances the energy the workforce as a whole is able to apply may diminish on a temporary basis. But where you as a leader have built strength in depth, and where momentum and direction of travel have been clearly established, you are able to ride through temporary difficulty. The built-up momentum carries you through. If, for example, a key member of staff leaves your team, such is the shared way of working and the clear understanding of 'the way you do things around here' that the team can absorb the temporary blip. No one is suggesting that maintaining high performance is easy, but what does seem to help is strength in depth built up over a number of years.

The best organisations are the result of a relentless and focused effort sustained over time

The best organisations are the result of a relentless and focused effort sustained over time where all stakeholders are consistently pushing in the same direction; they represent an aligned implementation of policy where success breeds success and where it becomes hard for everyone to resist joining in and becoming part of the story.

Nudges

- How good is your own personal effectiveness?

- How do you know? Could using a 360 be a useful way to get feedback on this?

- Might adopting the email-based task and prioritisation system be useful in your context?

- Does Jim Collins' fly-wheel concept resonate in your context?

Speak your mind when you need to

You're not learning anything unless you're having the difficult conversations.

GWYNETH PALTROW

Gwyneth Paltrow began acting as a child. In 1995, she appeared in the controversial film Se7en, alongside Morgan Freeman and Brad Pitt. From there, Paltrow won starring roles in a string of films and in 1999 won an Oscar for Best Actress for her role in *Shakespeare in Love*. Paltrow later appeared in *Iron Man* (2008) and was married to Coldplay frontman Chris Martin from 2003 to 2016.

Straightforward, honest conversations are an important element of effective accountability. They really can make everyone's job easier and your workplace better. Organisations with clear accountability structures, systems and cycles, with excellent quality assurance at every level, achieve great things.

But accountability has to be fair, mutually agreed, understood and consistent if it is to achieve optimum impact. Being held to account, when done well, should feel like a positive and rewarding experience. From the perspective of one of your team members, for example, it is the feeling that you are clear about your role and responsibilities; you have been challenged by the requirements but have support in place if you need it. As you achieve benchmarks, you receive timely advice and constructive and helpful feedback and feel a sense of recognition and success when all has been achieved.

The diagram below summarises the characteristics of effective accountability.

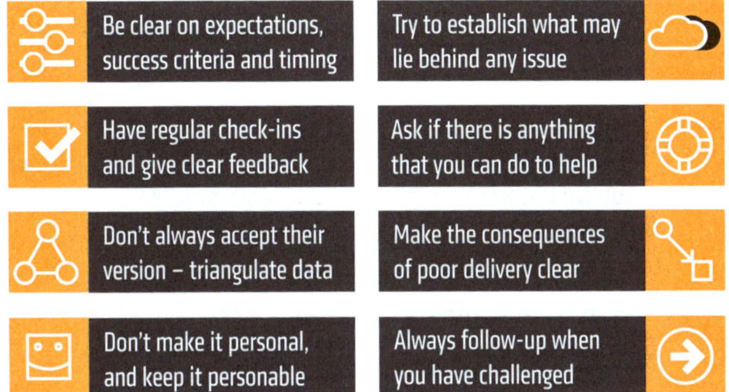

EFFECTIVE ACCOUNTABILITY

When accountability is used less wisely, it can create a fear factor in the workplace, community or organisation. If people are less clear on their role or responsibility, they do not feel ownership and are quick to blame others or cover up mistakes rather than be honest. Accountability at its best is constantly demanding the highest performance from every individual in the organisation, and people know what it looks like when their role is performed outstandingly well. If standards are not met, leaders are unafraid to look the person in the eye and say: 'this is not good enough', swift intervention is undertaken and consequences enforced. These conversations might not be easy, but we can give you some ideas about how to approach them.

When accountability is used less wisely,
it can create a fear factor in the workplace,
community or organisation

Systematising your processes can be very helpful. Try to be specific about what will be reviewed and when. Specify who will deliver the data or evidence required and outline the criteria for how its impact will be measured. Aim to provide people with a checklist of what should be achieved in a typical week, month, quarter or year for each role in their team.

In the case of staff appraisals, checking performance on a person-by-person basis is essential for good accountability. With this in place, how do you measure interim progress? What checks will you put in place to reassure yourself that you are on target and at which point should interventions, if necessary as a last resort, be put in place? A calendar and list of checkpoints should be shared with the success criteria clearly articulated. This is a transparent and shared way of measuring success. At a whole-company or organisation level, there may already be an established rhythm to this.

Having effective conversations about performance

Executive coach Susan Scott states that while no single conversation is guaranteed to change the trajectory of a career, a business or a life, any conversation has the capacity to do so.

When it comes to holding others to account, it can sometimes be useful to think about our conversations sitting within the simple continuum below.

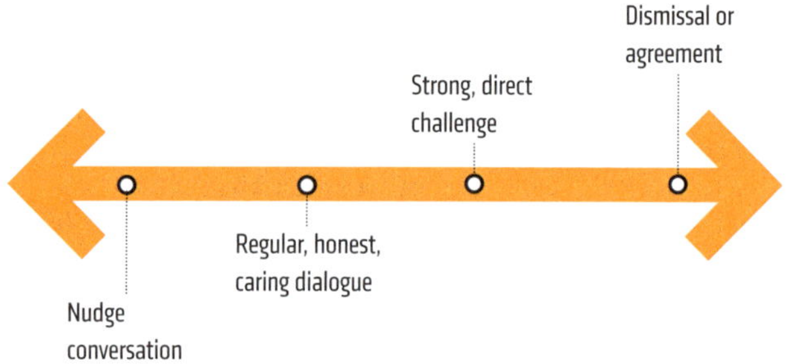

Nudge conversations

At one end of the spectrum are what we call nudge conversations, where you gently raise an issue. Sometimes this is achieved through making light of a situation with humour or mentioning an issue in passing. In most cases this can do the trick and the issue is resolved. By their very nature, these conversations are pretty easy to have.

Dismissal or agreement

At the other end of the spectrum are those conversations that lead to someone leaving your place of work. While harder than nudge conversations, these are still relatively easy as things will have become untenable and by then the decision is clearly the right thing to do. Often the person may not return to work, which again makes it a bit easier to manage. Of course, these situations need to be handled sensitively and appropriately, with individuals treated in a way that enables them to retain their personal dignity wherever possible.

Regular, honest, caring dialogue

As we have already seen, great conversations don't just involve you and your colleagues sharing ideas and debating issues. They sometimes involve disagreement or challenge, and this is a healthy feature of a great team. The trick, of course, is for this to not feel personal. It is about the idea or the behaviour not the person. It's about discovering the best way forward, not winning the argument. It's about the good of the team and what is best in the long run for your operation. Unfortunately, the *way* in which we sometimes disagree or challenge one another can increase the chances that someone will react defensively. Neil Pendle discourages meetings from getting heated; he encourages debate but wants his teams to find the best outcomes, which means his people need to be thinking clearly and not emotionally. He says: 'We are always looking for the best outcome and once the subject has been debated, the senior Director will have the final decision and we insist everybody then be on board.'

In her excellent book, *Radical Candor*, Kim Scott (2018) stresses the importance of leaders being able to have regular and honest conversations with colleagues about performance. But fundamental to her approach is the notion that these conversations need to be underpinned by trust and care; that the other person knows you care about them and want them to do well. The diagram below summarises her thinking.

KIM SCOTT

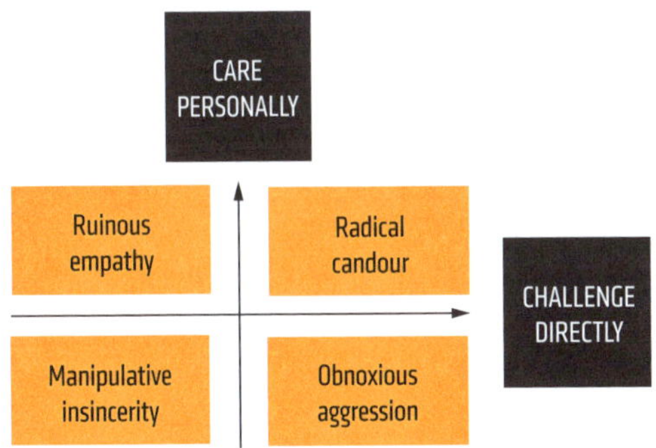

RADICAL CANDOUR MODEL
KIM SCOTT (2018)

Radical candour is the combination of challenging directly whilst showing you care about the individual, thus avoiding the risk of either:

- Ruinous empathy: this is often rooted in not wanting to upset people in the false belief that it will build effective relationships at work. In the end, people lose trust if all they ever get is positive feedback and no areas for development.

- Manipulative insincerity: when you don't care enough about the person to be straight with them and are only concerned with praising, just to be liked or gain political advantage.

- Obnoxious aggression: when you criticise without taking even a moment to show the person you care. Your approach will feel very unkind to the recipient.

One way we can minimise the chances of people getting personal and defensive is for us to mind our Ps and Qs. There are various theories about the origin of this phrase, but its meaning is pretty well understood: it's about being polite. So how can this help when it comes to robust debate in a meeting? The diagram below shows how the Ps and Qs model works.

MINDING YOUR PS AND QS

If you are good at offering feedback without people getting defensive, you probably already have the habit of focusing on the positive before asking a curious question. Taking this approach is usually much more likely to engender a response that gets colleagues *thinking* rather than *defending*.

Strong, direct challenge

The hardest conversations to have, the ones we tend to put off more than others, are those that are further along the continuum. You have tried nudging and it hasn't worked. You have 'minded your Ps and Qs' and still no response. These are the conversations where a direct challenge can be powerful.

CALLUM PETRIE

Callum Petrie, former HR Director for Philips UKI, South Africa and Nordics explains: 'Most people avoid difficult situations, it's human nature but if issues are not tackled the issue festers and can develop into a much larger issue. When I have asked managers why they avoid difficult conversations, a frequent response is that they feel ill equipped on how to approach the conversation and the situation. A key tool I offer managers and employees is to focus on how the other person's behaviour or actions make you feel. We all own our feelings and although others may disagree with how you should feel, they can't deny you feel them whereas if you use the "think" word it can be challenged as not being right or correct. Typically, I ask managers or employees about to embark on having a difficult conversation to say something like this: "Hi, (person's name) I would like to have a conversation about an issue that is concerning me. You are a good employee (positives first) but I want to talk about how I feel when you 'do X' (the issue in question) as when you 'do X' it makes me feel unappreciated/bullied/undermined (however it makes you feel) and I feel we need to change this situation, what do you think?" By saying the "feel" word it encourages the person to try and see the issue from your perspective, as remember they cannot deny how you feel.' This is clever and at *Honk!* we would encourage the use of this method as this especially resonates with us about the use of feelings and honesty.

Putting off conversations you dread usually only makes them worse

Putting off conversations you dread usually only makes them worse. Entrepreneur John Gehr suggests we should always 'deliver bad news fast and make sure it's to the point!' Once you have had a few (conversations, not glasses of wine), they do get easier.

JOHN GEHR

If you are about to have a difficult conversation, the work of Susan Scott – who is well known for her work in this area – in her book *Fierce Conversations – Achieving Success at Work and in Life One Conversation at a Time* (2003), suggests the opener to the conversation is critical. In the first (uninterrupted) sixty seconds, you should be very clear about what

SUSAN SCOTT

you are concerned about. She identifies seven clear steps which we have taken and evolved into a powerful acronym: NEFI ART. Inspired by Queen Nefertiti, this is explained below.

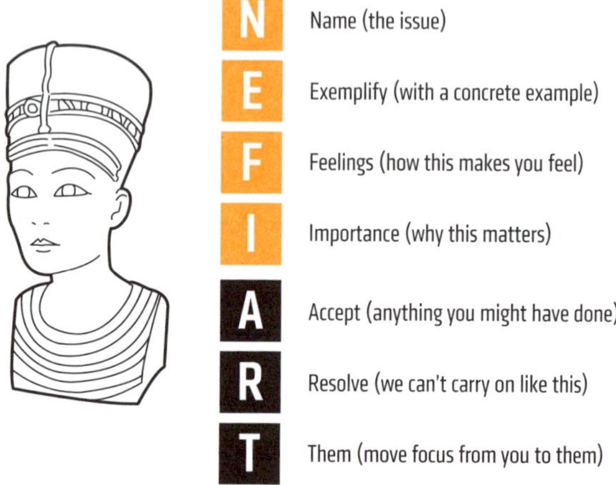

NEFI ART
INSPIRED BY SUSAN SCOTT

Critical to this process is making sure that once the situation has been set out, you do not go on to try to solve the issue until you have an acceptance from the other person of the validity of the concern. Unless someone has accepted their responsibility to change, they will simply pay lip service or change for a while but revert to their previous way of doing things.

This all sounds fine in theory, but you need to ensure that you are properly prepared not only to give this introduction, but also for what may follow. There might be a whole range of responses from silence or anger, to complete denial to emotional collapse. Thinking through in advance how you might respond to each of these can be helpful. Expect the unexpected.

Have you taken your brave pill?

Callum Petrie explains: 'In addition, a discussion needs to be as fact based as possible, performed in an air of openness and you must be prepared for the discussion to go in different directions with differing results than you maybe wanted. But in most cases the other person will not be enjoying the conversation either and will want to resolve the issue too once you have raised it. I always say to managers ahead of them having their difficult conversation "have you taken your brave pill?" What I am actually saying is, "have you prepared as per my guidance and will you focus on feeling over thinking?"'

You also need to try not to fall into the trap of 'propping up' the discussion that follows. Use questions to get the other person to talk and reflect on the issue, gain understanding and give a commitment to action. Let silences happen rather than be tempted to fill them. As Susan Scott suggests, let the silence do the heavy lifting. If the discussion goes off track, bring the dialogue back on to the issue you raised at the start. You need to keep in mind your overall approach to managing the issue. Remember that in having a difficult conversation you are in forcing, collaborating or compromising mode. You are not smoothing or avoiding. This can be particularly important if you know you have a tendency to gloss over issues in the hope that they will go away or be tackled another time. You need to be disciplined and you need to manage your own emotions, keeping to the facts at hand and the issue of concern.

You are not smoothing or avoiding

If the conversation has gone well, the other person will not only have clarity about the issue, they will often feel relieved that it is out in the open and that a way forward has been agreed. You will usually go away feeling relieved that you have done the hardest part, but do not forget the importance of monitoring the situation and offering support if needed.

Such discussions are serious, professional conversations. You cannot rely on or expect an existing friendship, personal loyalty or how long you have known and worked with someone to get you through such a meeting. On the other hand, you can't suddenly turn on 'seniority' mode and pull rank just to get your point across on a one-off occasion. Be empathetic, understanding and listen. Treat the recipient how you would wish to be treated if it were your line manager talking to you.

Allow the person to respond and, out of fairness, listen to what they say, but agree about the issue and some clear points for action. Finish with checking that they feel they have been treated fairly and where appropriate, clarify the action points in writing. It is important that the written part is supportive rather than seen as 'I am putting this in writing', which has different connotations. If the recipient feels you have been fair, feels what has been said is true, has a clear idea of how to respond and deliver and then does so, then you have managed a 'win-win' situation.

After a difficult conversation

After a difficult conversation it can be tempting to pretend it didn't happen, particularly if the person works closely with you. It can sometimes just be a bit awkward. The best thing is to be proactive and take steps to keep dialogue open. Thank them for the conversation and focus on the agreed outcomes positively, but don't forget to make sure you hold them to account for what they have agreed to. Finally, you may wish to get involved in an activity with the person that is nothing to do with what you have been discussing, maybe something you both enjoy.

The best thing is to be proactive and take steps to keep dialogue open

Moving people on

For most staff, even when performance drops, a good conversation and some high quality support can get a situation back on track. But there will be times, when it is obvious someone is not performing and has no intention or capacity to improve, when you need to be clear about moving them on. All organisations are required to have disciplinary and competency procedures, but in some they remain an underused vehicle for creating and maintaining high standards. There is nothing more frustrating for the hard-working and capable majority than to see a colleague who is not able or not interested in delivering to the desired standards being allowed to carry on unchallenged. Inevitably, if this situation is allowed to continue, other colleagues may start to become demotivated and their own standards will quickly begin to drop.

There is nothing more frustrating for the hard-working and capable majority than to see a colleague who is not able or not interested in delivering to the desired standards being allowed to carry on unchallenged

Of course, all colleagues are entitled to an appropriate level of confidentiality in such situations, but the staff body as a whole is usually very quick to recognise when action has been taken to deal with the underperformance of an individual. This can be a powerful motivator among the wider staff who see it as the role of leaders to ensure everyone on the team is delivering.

Over time, the culture in the workplace can change dramatically. As one of the outstanding organisations Andy has worked with describes: 'We have become increasingly confident in supportively yet assertively setting clear expectations for underperforming colleagues. Without ever needing to publicise the fact, other colleagues recognise that this is happening and see it as a positive rather than a threatening aspect of our approach.'

How the very best companies and organisations go about addressing issues of underperformance varies from place to place and from case to case. In some environments where a culture of high expectations is well established, simply beginning a competency procedure with a member of staff can often be sufficient for them to decide to move on. In other situations, particularly where a member of staff may have particularly long service, an organisation may have a more informal conversation around the particular circumstances of that individual's career stage. Increasingly, this may involve reaching an agreed financial settlement.

In all cases what all leaders should do is ensure that individuals that need it are offered 100% support in the first instance. Only if the required improvements fail to take place does it become necessary to consider the alternatives. This will involve working out an appropriate exit strategy and keeping to it.

IN ALL CASES WHAT ALL LEADERS SHOULD DO IS ENSURE THAT INDIVIDUALS THAT NEED IT ARE OFFERED 100% SUPPORT IN THE FIRST INSTANCE

The best organisations have real clarity about where they are in the process and avoid vacillating between trying to support and trying to remove someone. When all else has failed, they take decisive action and relentlessly pursue the goal to move someone on. This approach sounds somewhat draconian, but it is important to be clear about where you are in tackling an individual's underperformance.

Underperformance can go on for long periods where a place of work recognises the problem but almost unconsciously accepts it

In organisations where support is provided without clear targets and where a set period for performance review is not established, our own experience suggests such a lack of clarity can lead to a failure to take decisive action to remedy the situation. Underperformance can go on for long periods where a place of work recognises the problem but almost unconsciously accepts it. Your customers, stakeholders and colleagues deserve better than this.

Gabby Costigan, a former colonel in the Australian Army and now CEO of BAE Systems Australia says; 'I welcome challenging conversations, but once a decision has been reached, I expect co-operation. I don't tolerate those who don't buy in. Sometimes, you have to be very much, "we will be doing it this way."'

Nudges

- Do you have regular, honest, caring conversations with the people you line manage?

- Might you find it useful to 'Mind your Ps and Qs'?

- How good are you and your colleagues at having directly challenging conversations?

- Can you see the positive effect they can have?

- Might NEFI ART be a useful way to prepare and execute these conversations?

- Are you clear about your strategy at any given point in time when a colleague's performance is causing concern?

Prioritise for performance

STEPHEN COVEY

Stephen Covey was born on October 24, 1932 in Salt Lake City, Utah, USA. He was a writer, known for his best-selling works The *7 Habits of Highly Effective People* (1996) and *Jobbing* (2006). He was married to Sandra Merrill and died in 2012 from complications after a bicycle crash.

Taking time to step back from the day-to-day and reviewing your priorities is a great way to make sure you and your team are focusing on the right things. Get this right and you will all be more effective at achieving your goals.

If there's one thing all leaders have in common, it's the fact that it just seems like there's never enough time to do the job. Apart from managing the workload associated with your various teams, including monitoring and review, there's everything you are accountable for in your leadership role. But have you ever stopped and really thought about what you do with your time, or thought about whether there are things you could do to ease the burden and make things more efficient? And don't forget this doesn't just apply to you, it applies to all your staff, whatever their role, so it's vital that you lead by example. Ensuring staff have manageable workloads is a key action leaders need to take and is vital in building discretionary effort and increasing retention rates. We think it's interesting here to take a step sideways and look at how others handle this necessary skill.

Ensuring staff have manageable workloads is a key action leaders need to take and is vital in building discretionary effort and increasing retention rates

Approaches to managing time

The reality is that people have very different approaches to the use of time. Some people are actually energised by deadlines and find it most productive to work right up to them. Others can't bear the thought of having everything left until the last minute and will want everything planned out well in advance. Then there are those who just can't say 'no' when a job comes up, but who never stop to ask themselves whether they have time to do everything they have agreed to. Others are great procrastinators who will always find something else to do other than the things they really should be doing. Finally, there are those who just have to spend the time to get the detail right, even if that means other things are delayed or stress levels rise.

You probably know leaders that fit all these descriptions, and you might find it interesting to reflect on your own predispositions in this respect. For all leaders, when it comes to better time management, knowing your own predispositions can be helpful.

FOR ALL LEADERS, WHEN IT COMES TO BETTER TIME MANAGEMENT, KNOWING YOUR OWN PREDISPOSITIONS CAN BE HELPFUL

Senior police leader Sue Scott says she's probably a hybrid of all of the above and her style was underpinned by her bounding enthusiasm to get involved in as much as possible because she enjoyed being able to assist and influence what was going on. Her key to managing her time while taking on so much was her ability to delegate and empower her team members, sharing her enthusiasm and being inclusive. She notes that in her last two years at the top she had a PA who was fantastic; they worked well together and Sue insisted that her PA use her own initiative and make decisions.

So what can you actually do to manage your time more effectively? To start with you may want to log how you spend your time over the course of a typical week. This will give you an idea about how much time you spend in each of the three circles in the leadership model below. Typically, experience tells us that leaders – particularly in the public sector – find their time being sucked into the *Deliver* circle, with insufficient time devoted to the equally important areas of *Future* and *Engage*.

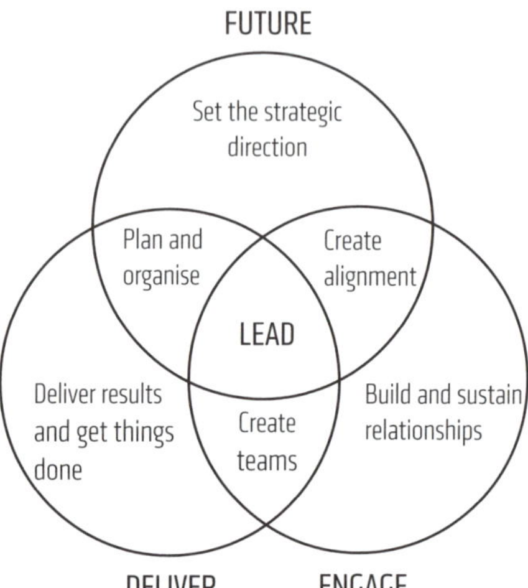

SIX KEY AREAS FOR LEADERSHIP ACTION
ADAPTED FROM DAVID PENDLETON'S PRIMARY COLOURS MODEL AND STEVE RADCLIFFE'S FUTURE-ENGAGE-DELIVER

We can achieve 80% of a result from 20% of effort

You may also want to reflect on the Pareto Principle. Basically, what this helpfully reminds us is that typically we can achieve 80% of a result from 20% of effort. To achieve the same task perfectly takes a disproportionately larger amount of time (the remaining 80%). Just consider for a moment, the difference in taking on five tasks and giving them 20% effort (thus achieving a result of 400%) versus just doing one thing perfectly (resulting in a 100% result). One is clearly far more efficient.

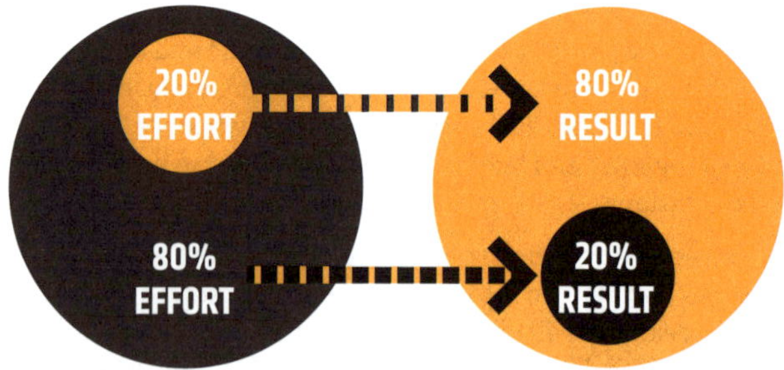

THE PARETO PRINCIPLE
KOCH (1998)

While this clearly won't translate exactly to every goal we have, there is something worth reflecting on here. If you have the habit of wanting everything to be perfect, you may be being less efficient than you could be. Of course, there are some things that need to be 100% right, we are not suggesting you get the books to roughly balance, for example, or thinking back to the airline pilot from earlier, 80% of landings being successful would not be great. But we do think there is something we can learn from this approach.

Practical action

There are some simple practical things that can help you and your team. You probably do many of these already, but how ruthless are you in carrying them out? It is precisely when the pressure starts to build that most people tend to throw logic and reason out of the window and just respond to things as they arrive on their desk.

Goal setting

Set yourself goals. These are not the same as to-do lists, they are strategic things you and your team want to achieve in a given time frame and they should drive your overall planning. It might be helpful to break them down into small manageable chunks. You need to be realistic when setting your goals, there is nothing more satisfying than meeting your goals and nothing more frustrating than always failing to achieve them.

Set yourself goals. These are not the same as to-do lists

Just say no

If you are one of those people who just can't say 'no', then learn to, you'll be surprised how quickly people find someone else to ask. It's sometimes worth explaining why you can't help and maybe suggesting options of where the person can go – in the nicest possible way of course.

Schedule time for the important but not urgent

It can be helpful to plan out when you are going to get certain things done. Not only does this help with the temptation to put things off, it means you can let others know what you are doing. This can be important if you find too much of your time is spent dealing with 'incidents' that maybe others can help with on a rota basis. It will also help reduce interruptions, particularly if you combine this with something as simple as saying to your team that if your door is closed, you would prefer not to be interrupted.

IT CAN BE HELPFUL TO PLAN OUT WHEN YOU ARE GOING TO GET CERTAIN THINGS DONE

Avoid procrastination; eat your frog!

If you are prone to putting things off, you need to develop ways that help you get down to business. Often, the hardest part is just getting started. There is a school of thought that says you should try to make the very first thing you do each day the thing you are least looking forward to doing. The idea is that you immediately feel pleased once this task is done and are consequently much more efficient and energised than you would be if the job you are dreading were still hanging over you. Try it, it really works. We'd suggest that this dreaded item is often the most important one on your list too so to knock it over first is an all-round win. You can also search for 'Eat the Frog' on YouTube to see a short video on this.

Make the very first thing you do each day the thing you are least looking forward to doing

Set time limits

If you are prone to just working until the job gets done, you can be sure you will have absolutely no work-life balance. If this is your tendency, set yourself strict time limits and make sure you stick to them. If that means something will have to wait until tomorrow, then so be it.

Delegate more

This is easy to say and hard to do but there are lots of ideas in Chapter 13. How often do you ask yourself if someone else could do a particular task? If you do, how often do you decide not to ask someone to do something because you think:

- others are just as busy as you

- they aren't paid to do this

- they won't do it as well or as quickly as you

- someone might think you are shirking your responsibilities?

OFTEN PEOPLE MAKE ALL KINDS OF ASSUMPTIONS ABOUT WHAT OTHERS ARE THINKING OR ARE PREPARED TO DO

All these reactions are typical and sometimes true. But often people make all kinds of assumptions about what others are thinking or are prepared to do. You will be surprised how carefully chosen tasks, planned in advance, can be seen by others as a great opportunity to develop and make an important contribution to the team. The key is to do this in a way that doesn't seem like you are just dumping a problem on someone else at the last minute because you can't be bothered to do it or haven't planned properly.

A model for prioritisation

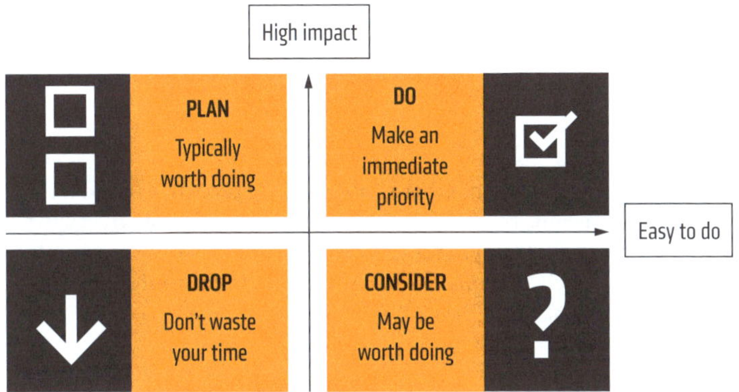

A MODEL FOR PRIORITISATION
ADAPTED FROM VARMA

Do

These are your classic win-wins. Easy to do and have a big impact: why wouldn't you do them?

Drop

These are the things that are hard to do and make little difference: why on earth are you still doing these? The answer is sometimes because someone else has asked you to. Time to have a *managing up* conversation.

Plan

These are things which will make a big difference but are hard to do. A good strategy is to plan ahead, breaking the task into more manageable chunks and celebrating at each step along the way. These tasks also require you to block out larger chunks of time and do all you can to protect that time.

Consider

These are easy to do tasks, but they don't make that much difference. You might want to do some of them, after all, ticking off a few things on the to-do list is good for the soul. Andy said that when he was a teacher, he would spend 20 minutes at the end of a day on a Friday fiddling with his classroom displays. It wasn't going to transform his teaching, but it did help create a welcoming environment for pupils and he found it a very therapeutic end to his week. The key here is not doing jobs in this box at the expense of those in the hard to do but high impact top left box.

Take control and discover how much more is possible when you set yourself some simple but important goals to achieve

So effective time management is all about being proactive in the way you use this precious commodity. Don't allow yourself to be the victim of your circumstances or your own predispositions. Take control and discover how much more is possible when you set yourself some simple but important goals to achieve.

MICK reviews

One organisation we have worked with uses a very simple tool to review with staff how they could be more effective when it comes to time. Every quarter they give all employees the chance to contribute to a MICK review:

M — **MORE** What is working well and we should do more of?

I — **INCLUDE** What would help us achieve our goals that we couldn't currently do?

C — **CHANGE** What do we do that is important bit not quite working at the moment?

K — **KICK-OUT** What do we do at the moment that we could probably manage without?

What is powerful about this model is that it allows staff a voice to feed back to more senior team members about what might be in the *Drop* box in the prioritisation model as well as encouraging innovation and recognition of what is important to keep doing or improving.

Nudges

- Does the Pareto principle resonate in your context?

- Does it make sense to you to get the 'dreaded item' off your list first?

- Could the prioritisation grid be useful in identifying how you could be more effective?

- Could the MICK review idea be useful in your context?

Create change that sticks

PETER SENGE

Peter Senge was born in 1947, he studied engineering at Stanford and
went on to undertake a masters in social systems modelling at MIT
before completing his PhD in management. He is the founding chair
of the Society for Organisational Learning.

How you manage change with your team or organisation
can make a big difference to what you can achieve
together. Handled well, people understand why a
change is necessary and are motivated to try something new.
Successful change is all about making things better for the
long term.

At its heart, the role of any leader is all about making change
happen, not just for a while but for the long term. Whether
that be improving the performance of a colleague in a
particular area of practice, or designing and implementing
a new policy, the key to the success of any change is that
it sticks. Too often in an organisation someone focuses
on improving something, but not for long enough or in a
sufficiently systematic way to ensure a change is embedded
that will have a long term impact on customer or stakeholder
outcomes.

Similarly, when it comes to developing a new policy or approach, an
individual can sometimes introduce a new idea without properly engaging
with those who will be responsible for making it happen or really thinking
through how it will be implemented in practice. Before long the idea has
withered on the vine or, at best, is being inconsistently applied.

Change is probably one of the most important, challenging and difficult problems facing any business

So how do you approach changing things in a way that will bring about sustainable impact for your team? There are numerous theories about how to 'do' change. John Gannon points out: 'Change is probably one of the most important, challenging and difficult problems facing any business. I have seen over the years many loyal, productive, effective people come completely unstuck because they were unable to cope with change or new processes.'

Many ideas for change originate with leadership and change management guru John Kotter. A professor at Harvard Business School and world-renowned change expert, Kotter introduced his eight-step change process in his 1996 book *Leading Change*.

EIGHT STEPS OF CHANGE
JOHN KOTTER (1996)

Step one: increase urgency

For change to happen, it helps if the whole team or organisation really wants it. So how do you engage staff when there is a natural resistance to change? How do you develop a sense of urgency around the need for change? It isn't simply a matter of you telling staff about the demands of yet another initiative or performance goal, showing them the latest sales targets or scaring them with new KPIs. It is about you instigating an open, honest and convincing dialogue about what's happening in the business landscape within your context. You might decide it would be useful to identify potential problems that lie ahead if things don't change, and develop scenarios showing what could happen in the future. However you achieve this, you need to start honest discussions and give dynamic and convincing reasons to get people talking and thinking.

For change to happen, it helps if the whole team or organisation really wants it

Step two: build a 'change team'

As with any whole-organisation change, if time permits it's a good idea to get a small group of people to work up your ideas. Using your change team to help develop your plans is useful in itself, but having them as a small group of advocates for change, communicating with the rest of the team can be very powerful, particularly if you have managed to include one or two key influencers.

Having them as a small group of advocates for change, communicating with the rest of the team can be very powerful

If you are leading across more than one company or location, steps one and two in Kotter's model are particularly important if you are going to gain the traction you are likely to need. John Gannon suggests: 'Delivering change effectively is all about execution. You can have the best planned, prepared and communicated change management process going, however it's up to individual line managers and ultimately the chief exec of an organisation to ensure that everyone is on board and pulling in the one direction.'

Step three: get the vision right

When you first start thinking about change, there will probably be many great ideas and solutions floating around. You need to link these concepts to an overall vision that people can grasp easily and remember. A clear vision can help everyone understand why you're asking them to do something. When people see for themselves what you're trying to achieve, then the directives they're given tend to make more sense.

Consulting on the vision for a change can also be a good way for you to help generate interest in making it work.

Step four: communication for buy-in

What you and your change team do with your plans after they have been created is crucial. Your message will probably have strong competition from other day-to-day pressures and priorities, so you need to communicate it frequently and powerfully, and embed it within everything you do. You need to keep telling the story. John Gannon suggests that recognition and reward for people who do question how a task is being done is important. Proactively seek recommendations or suggestions for change from people. Make it fun, offer incentives at all levels for people to consider how and why they would make changes to the current workplace.

You need to keep telling the story

Involving line managers and staff in this stage can be a powerful way of building buy-in for an idea, it also helps people see the benefits for customers or stakeholders in ways they may not have quite appreciated before.

It's also important for you, as the driver of the change, to 'walk the talk'. What you do is often far more important – and believable – than what you say. You should demonstrate the kind of behaviour you want from others.

Step five: enable action

If you follow the steps and reach this point in the change process, you've already been talking about the vision and building buy-in. Hopefully, staff want to get busy and achieve the benefits that you have been promoting. But is anyone resisting the change? And are there processes or structures getting in its way?

It's important to identify and put in place the structure for change, and continually check for barriers to it. Removing obstacles can empower the people you need to execute the vision, and can help the change move forward. One way to do this is to delegate to mini-teams. At a more senior level, using sub-teams to deliver on a change can be a great way of playing to strengths and keeping things manageable. People at all levels within an organisation must be encouraged and challenged to consider if how they are working is the most efficient way of doing so and management must create the environment and the catalyst to promote this challenging process.

Step six: create short term wins

Nothing motivates more than success

Nothing motivates more than success. Look out for ways you can give your staff a taste of victory early in the change process. This could be a month or a year, depending on the type of change, but they'll want to have results they can see. Without this, critics and negative thinkers might impact on your progress. People need to be thinking that the change is a good thing and they need to feel the benefits fast.

Many change projects fail because victory is declared too early

Step seven: don't let up

Kotter argues that many change projects fail because victory is declared too early. Real change runs deep, and quick wins are only the beginning of what needs to be done to achieve long term change. You need to tackle those who don't appear to be on board. Typically, these stragglers are the last to adopt any change, but if you have spent time properly defining how the change will work at stages two and three, then these are easy conversations to have. And remember, you also need to be fully behind the change you are driving, there is nothing worse than saying to someone that they need to make a change when you know deep down it isn't 100% the right thing to be doing.

EACH SUCCESS YOU HAVE PROVIDES AN OPPORTUNITY TO BUILD ON WHAT WENT RIGHT AND IDENTIFY WHAT CAN BE IMPROVED

Each success you have provides an opportunity to build on what went right and identify what can be improved. It can be helpful to take time to reflect, as a team, on 'what went well' and what might be 'even better if ...'. This will help to flick that switch in their heads and help them to see that change is good and can be a positive part of your workplace culture.

Step eight: make it stick

Finally, to make any change stick, it should become part of your culture and be consistently applied. Your monitoring systems should now place a value on the things you have changed to help embed them and the key milestones should be part of the wider team or organisation's development plan. How you recognise and celebrate success, both as an organisation and as a team, will reflect the changes you have made.

Enabling action

Stage five of Kotter's model is about making sure there is nothing to stop a change being successful; it's about making sure all the key ingredients for a successful change are in place. This is where Kotter's model overlaps usefully with another change model from Knoster, Thousand and Villa (2000):

VISION	SKILLS	INCENTIVES	RESOURCES	ACTION PLANS	SUCCESS
	Skills	Incentives	Resources	Action Plans	CONFUSION
Vision		Incentives	Resources	Action Plans	ANXIETY
Vision	Skills		Resources	Action Plans	SLOW CHANGE
Vision	Skills	Incentives		Action Plans	FRUSTRATION
Vision	Skills	Incentives	Resources		FALSE STARTS

DIMENSIONS OF CHANGE
KNOSTER, THOUSAND AND VILLA
(2000)

As the model suggests, if one key element is missing it will have consequences. By combining the two models, we have come up with what we call our Checklist for Change.

ACTION	WHEN	NOTES
Be clear why change is needed — get people wanting change		
Get a small group working on it and review the evidence of what works		
Create a draft vision and proposal		
Test it out with people		
Make sure everything is in place (especially skills and time to do it)		
Launch		
Ensure quick wins		
Get real-time feedback		
Challenge those not adopting		
Build into standard routines for planning and evaluation		

Managing the effect of change on others

People respond differently to change, but we all go through a series of stages of how we feel about it. Our feelings of self-worth or competence can be affected and it is not uncommon for people to doubt they can perform successfully in the way a change may demand. The most commonly known model for illustrating how this happens was developed by Elisabeth Kübler-Ross in 1969:

It is not uncommon for people to doubt they can perform successfully in the way a change may demand

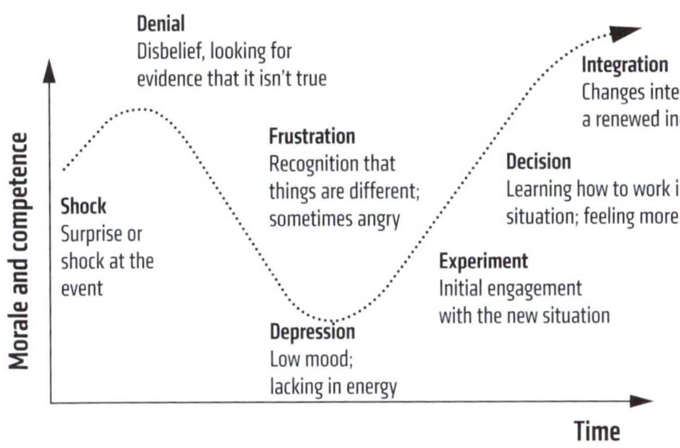

THE CHANGE CURVE
ADAPTED FROM THE KÜBLER-ROSS MODEL

When you are introducing a significant change, it is well worth taking some time to think about how the individuals in the team are likely to react and then work out the best way to approach things with them, without compromising your overall goals. It's important to plan but not to overcomplicate a change management process because the biggest hurdle will be gaining acceptance from those resistant to it. As a company, you may wish to use one of the personality predisposition tools available, such as those we have developed at *Honk!* to support this. Once again, this is about understanding your situation before acting.

Keep the change you want to make as simple as possible

In addition to using Kotter's eight-step model as a useful guide to thinking about change and thinking about how different team members may respond to it, you may also want to consider these points:

- Keep the change you want to make as simple as possible. This makes it easier to communicate, easier to get buy-in, easier to deliver consistently and easier to monitor in terms of impact.

- When you consult on a change, you should remember to thank everyone who has taken the time to give you feedback and welcome their input, even though some of it may be negative. Giving people a proper chance to get things off their chest can be an important part of the change process.

- After consultation, always make sure you feed back what you have heard. Where you have decided not to act on a particular point, you should take the time to explain why. This is often best done face-to-face. It is important for people to feel they have been heard, even if, in the end, their argument hasn't won the day (from our experience, middle managers aren't always good at this).

- You should be prepared to be flexible, but only if by doing so you can take more people with you and still make the change you want to make. Showing flexibility can also be important if the change you have made doesn't appear to have been successful. If, after a sufficient period of time, there is clear evidence that the whole team has worked hard for a change, but it isn't delivering the impact you had hoped, it is a sign of strength to acknowledge this and find another way forward.

Nudges

- Do you and colleagues use any models to help you plan change?

- Do you recognise resistance to change?

- How might you involve your whole team in change decisions to reduce resistance?

- Might using or creating a checklist for change be useful?

Ask first, every time

> 'Tain't what you do
> (It's the way that you do it).

MELVIN OLIVER AND JAMES YOUNG
This song was written by jazz musicians Melvin 'Sy' Oliver and James
'Trummy' Young. It was first recorded in 1939 by Jimmie Lunceford,
Harry James, and Ella Fitzgerald.

Doing the right thing is an essential prerequisite for great leadership; the actions we take as leaders will ultimately define our success. But as the saying goes, it's not just what you do but the way you do it that matters. Your approach to what you do can make a real difference.

In many ways, getting this right boils down to two things:

- Knowing your own predispositions and how you tend to approach things when you are on auto-pilot.

- Thinking about the leadership style the people or context need from you at any given moment.

Asking first is a powerful technique to support both these aims, but before we explore its potential, let's take a closer look at what we mean by leadership styles. By the end of the chapter you will hopefully see why asking first is such a powerful way to ensure you use the right leadership style in all your conversations.

Leadership style

So what do we mean by leadership style? Why does leadership style matter? Are some leadership styles more effective than others? Daniel Goleman, who is probably best known for his work on emotional intelligence, also investigated the impact of leadership style on the climate of organisations. His findings support our ideas at *Honk!* where we believe the best leaders and managers will develop the most flexibility in their style to get the best outcomes from their people.

Leadership style is not about good or bad, or right and wrong, but rather it depends on the task, people and situation involved. The key to being an effective leader is to have a broad repertoire of styles and use them appropriately.

THE KEY TO BEING AN EFFECTIVE LEADER IS TO HAVE A BROAD REPERTOIRE OF STYLES AND USE THEM APPROPRIATELY

The best leaders and managers will develop the most flexibility in their style to get the best outcomes from their people

In Daniel Goleman's 2000 paper *Leadership that gets results* he identified that, as leaders, we tend to use the following six different leadership styles:

Visionary (sometimes called authoritative)

Primary objective: providing long term direction and vision. You tend to:

- develop and articulate a clear vision

- solicit staff perspectives on the vision and see selling the vision as key to success

- persuade staff by explaining the rationale for the team's best long term interests

- set standards and monitor performance in relation to the wider vision

- motivate with a balance of positive and negative feedback.

Affiliative

Primary objective: creating staff harmony. You tend to:

- be concerned with promoting friendly interactions

- place more emphasis on addressing staff needs than on goals and standards

- pay attention to, and care for, the whole person; stress things that keep people happy

- avoid performance related confrontations

- reward personal characteristics more than job performance.

Directive (sometimes called coercive)

Primary objective: compliance. You tend to:

- give lots of directives, not direction
- expect immediate staff compliance
- control tightly
- rely on negative, corrective feedback
- motivate by imposing sanctions for non-compliance, with few rewards
- rarely explain rationale, only negative consequences.

Democratic

Primary objective: building commitment and generating new ideas. You tend to:

- trust that staff can develop the appropriate direction for themselves and the organisation
- invite staff to participate in decisions
- reach decisions by consensus
- delegate decision making as well as tasks
- hold many meetings and listen to staff concerns
- reward adequate performance; rarely give negative feedback.

Pace-setting

Primary objective: making rapid progress and achieving tasks to high standards of excellence. You tend to:

- lead by example and have high standards: 'look at me; do what I am doing; keep up with me'
- expect others to know the rationale behind what is being modelled
- are apprehensive about delegating
- take responsibility away if high performance is not forthcoming, and have little sympathy for poor performance
- rescue the situation or give detailed task instructions when staff experience difficulties.

Coaching

Primary objective: long term professional development of others. You tend to:

- help staff identify their unique strengths and weaknesses

- encourage staff to establish long range development goals

- reach agreement with staff on the team leader's and individuals' roles in the development process

- provide on-going advice and feedback

- sometimes trade off immediate standards of performance for long term development.

As you reflect upon the six styles, do you think there is one you tend to predominantly use? Which do you rarely use? Do you make a conscious effort to think about the right approach for any given situation or do you rely on gut instinct?

Sometimes a team can need a very directional approach from a leader

Sometimes a team can need a very directional approach from a leader, particularly if it isn't functioning well. If you are working with individuals who are not operating as a unit and where performance is variable, you may just need to say: 'we need to do it like this'. Getting the basics in place has to be the priority. If the situation in which you find yourself is in disarray, setting clear expectations with a back to basics approach will help you find a starting point, and to do this you may need to be fairly directive to start with.

A high performing team would find such an approach completely de-motivating, and coming in and telling people what to do would be a disaster. You need to reflect upon the capacity, competence and experience of your team. Knowing which style is best used with the team as a whole, or with individuals within it, is where your professional judgement and emotional awareness as a leader come in. What is important is that you take the time to consciously think about which approach will build discretionary effort and have the impact you are seeking.

YOU NEED TO REFLECT UPON THE CAPACITY, COMPETENCE AND EXPERIENCE OF YOUR TEAM

We have summarised each of Goleman's six styles and when it might be appropriate to use each.

STYLE	DESCRIPTION	WHEN USEFUL	CORRELATION
Visionary	Communicating the goal; expectations on delivery	Pretty much anytime; set pieces and 1:1 dialogue	+54
Affiliative	Building and sustaining relationships	Again, always useful but especially if morale is poor	+46
Directive	Telling people what to do, often in detail	Low capability or competence; no time	-26
Democratic	Sharing decision making; delegating power	Confidence in the team; more time available	+43
Pace-setting	Copy me and keep up with me	When you need fast change; show what's possible	-25
Coaching	Asking questions; focus on developing others	When you have the time to build capacity in others	+42

SUMMARY OF DIFFERENT LEADERSHIP STYLES AND WHEN TO USE THEM
BASED ON GOLEMAN (2000)

Goleman's work looked at the overall effectiveness of each of the six leadership styles. However, as the final column showing the correlation of each factor with a positive climate shows, it appears that two leadership styles can have a negative effect. Goleman identified that the directive and pace-setting leadership styles had a negative impact on climate in the long term, even though there are times when they are absolutely the right approaches to take. The damaging impact would be more likely if for a prolonged period of time these styles are overly-relied upon at the expense of the others. This is not really a surprise; if, as a leader, you find yourself constantly leading by example or telling people what to do because you need to, you are working with people who maybe aren't suited to their roles and need to either improve fast or 'get off the bus'. On the other hand, if you are using these styles but don't actually need to, you will be leading a team who feel you don't trust them and probably feel micromanaged.

The directive and pace-setting leadership styles had a negative impact on climate in the long term

As the data shows, Goleman also identified that the visionary and affiliative leadership styles were, on average, the most effective overall, closely followed by the democratic and coaching styles. However, a degree of caution has to be applied when using correlations like this, not least because the figures shown here are not always statistically significant. With your own team it's a good idea to reflect on their personalities and work out which management style will suit each individual best in terms of their professional development.

Fergal reflects that on his 11-year journey of running The Key, from start-up to maturity, his leadership style carried different blends during this time. In the early days there was a fair mix of the visionary, and far too much of the democratic. A couple of the management team were quite political in their thinking and Fergal accommodated this by allowing long weekly meetings where all decisions were made by the team. Although this was great for getting everyone on board, it meant that decision making was far too slow for much of the time. When government funding was lost, there followed a period of pace-setting mixed with affiliative, always with a strong visionary drive underneath. When investors were brought into the business, the lead investor challenged Fergal as to why he consulted so much. Was he scared of making decisions? Fergal responded by being much more explicit as to his intentions, although his natural disposition was always to make sure that the management team were as one when it came to major decisions. It was always clear to him that the chair (who was also the lead investor) would have preferred him to have taken a more directive approach, with the assumption that this would have led to quicker decisions, but this was far from Fergal's natural style. In his last two years with the company and with an exceptionally strong management team, Fergal's style was heavily dependent on a coaching model, as he tried to make strong people stronger.

Individual, team and organisational journeys

Taking a moment to think about your leadership approach – and in particular the right style for your current context or situation – has the potential to make a big difference to the discretionary effort in your team. When it comes to thinking about the typical journey of improvement most individuals, teams and organisations go through, we have come up with the simple model set out below.

ALTHOUGH THIS WAS GREAT FOR GETTING EVERYONE ON BOARD, IT MEANT THAT DECISION MAKING WAS FAR TOO SLOW FOR MUCH OF THE TIME

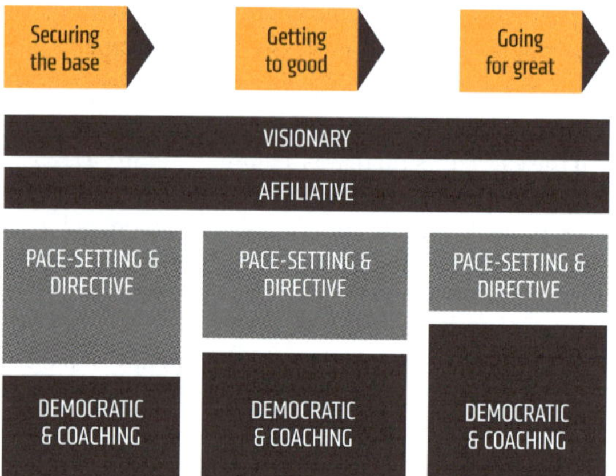

CHANGING LEADERSHIP STYLE OVER TIME

In all three stages, remembering that a visionary and affiliative leadership style will probably be useful in all contexts is a useful reminder in itself, but the degree to which you need to be pace-setting and directive ought to decline over time. In tandem with this you should be gradually increasing how much you use the democratic and coaching leadership styles.

The challenge for leaders at all levels is recognising when the context you are working in has evolved, and then adapting your style to suit the change. Too often, leaders can get stuck with the leadership habits that served them well at the start of the journey and fail to make the necessary adjustments along the way. Flexibility in your approach is key, coupled with the ability to focus on the bigger picture to make sure that you are steering the ship the right way at all times and in all weathers.

Leaders can get stuck with the leadership habits that served them well at the start of the journey

Asking first

So how can 'asking first' help you to adopt the right leadership approach?

In the end, using the right leadership style is about developing the right habits. When colleagues come to you to ask for help with something, you probably only have three types of conversation, as set out below. The thickness of the arrow indicates the relative frequency with which you may wish to have these conversations in the longer term.

The right leadership style is about developing the right habits

'Monkey on the shoulder' conversations

In the first type of conversation, before you know it, you've ended up with a job. We call these your 'monkey on the shoulder' conversations where the monkey has quickly jumped from the other person on to you. Of course, there is a time and place that this is appropriate. If something is high risk and looking like it is about to go wrong, you may well need to step in. If a colleague is really stressed for some reason and just can't cope, you need to help. But if your habit is to take on jobs from others without thinking, you aren't really leading, you are just doing.

Andy recalls that as a young head of year in school, he let a huge number of monkeys jump on his back. On reflection there were a number of reasons why this tended to happen: because he genuinely wanted to help out someone who he thought was very busy; because he wanted the other person to think he was capable and good at his job; because it often felt, as he has mentioned before, that it would be quicker and easier to do something himself; and finally, because the reality of the culture in that school at the time was that heads of year were seen as firefighters, not team leaders. But as the thickness of the arrow on the model implies, while there is a place for type one conversations, you shouldn't have too many.

If something is high risk and looking like it is
about to go wrong, you may well need to step in

'Wise owl' conversations

The second type of conversation also has its place. These are dialogues in which you end up giving advice, making suggestions or even just telling someone what to do. At least with these, you don't end up doing the job, and hopefully the other person will be able to apply what they have learned from the conversation in the future. But if they keep coming back to you with similar questions, and if you continue to just answer them, they can become over-dependent upon you when it comes to making decisions. In this situation, these conversations don't build capacity or competence in your colleagues. In fact, they do the reverse.

If you continue to just answer them, they can
become over-dependent upon you

'Dolphin' conversations

In type three conversations, you just ask brilliant questions. Initially, these help you understand the situation; both the context and an individual's capacity to manage it. Only then can you decide how best to proceed. If at this point you need to intervene and take the job off them or give them advice, then that's fine. You have made a conscious decision to do that, not because it's what you are predisposed to do, but because it's what the situation needs. There is also the added benefit that the quality of your advice will be better because you know more about the situation.

Of course, if you both have time, spending a tiny bit longer on the conversation and staying in questioning mode can very often help people work out for themselves what they need to do. These mini-coaching conversations don't have to take long; it's more about you using a coaching leadership style than it is actually formal coaching.

You will be surprised, even in a three-minute conversation, how much of this ground can be covered. You leave the conversation with no task to undertake. Your colleague leaves feeling they have been properly

STAYING IN QUESTIONING MODE
CAN VERY OFTEN HELP PEOPLE
WORK OUT FOR THEMSELVES
WHAT THEY NEED TO DO

listened to and having had the opportunity to think through the situation. They are also less likely to ask you the same question again next time.

If you are wondering why we have called these 'dolphin' conversations, we have to confess the rationale is somewhat tenuous. Basically, we wanted to keep the animal analogy going and we like dolphins! They also look rather like a question mark when jumping through the air with an inflatable ball.

Asking first

So how does *asking first* help us use the right leadership approach? To answer this, we need to first of all see the connection between these three conversations and Goleman's six leadership styles. Type one conversations are effectively about acting in a pace-setting style. Type two, where we offer advice is more akin to being directive. Type three conversations are more of a blend of democratic and coaching leadership styles. Visionary and affiliative probably to apply to all three.

If you *start* all your conversations by asking great questions, you are giving colleagues the chance to work out their own solutions. If you subsequently realise that they aren't able to work out what to do (or if time is short) you may decide you need to give some advice or show them what to do. That's absolutely fine. You are consciously using the leadership approach that suits the situation, rather than just diving in with advice or taking the job from them.

In other words, by asking first in all your conversations, without even thinking about it, you have a much greater chance of adopting the right leadership approach in every conversation you have.

Nudges

- Have you developed a range of leadership styles that you use flexibly with different colleagues?

- Are there situations which would benefit from you using a different leadership style? What about people?

- Do you tend to just use one or two styles rather than the full range?

- Have you or your colleagues changed style over time to suit any change in context?

- Have you changed your style to work with certain individuals or customers or suppliers?

- Are you aware of the balance of type one, two and three conversations you have?

- Do you already have the habit of *asking first* or is this something you want to focus on?

Be great to talk to

It is more fun to talk with someone who doesn't use long, difficult words but rather short, easy words, like 'What about lunch?'

A. A. MILNE

Born in 1882, Alan Alexander Milne was a British author, best known for his books about the teddy bear Winnie-the-Pooh. Milne was a noted writer, primarily as a playwright, before the huge success of Pooh overshadowed his previous work. He served in both World Wars, joining the British Army in World War I, and was a captain of the British Home Guard in World War 2.

So what's it like to talk to you? Do you leave people feeling positive and energetic about the future? Or have you cast rather a cloud over proceedings, leaving them feeling less confident or excited about what lies ahead? Thinking about how you engage with others in everyday conversations can make a big difference to how they perform at work.

If you plan to use the *asking first* strategy from the previous chapter, then this chapter is for you. We will explore what great coaching conversations can look like, both in terms of structure and approach.

In Chapter 19, we looked at the three types of conversations that we suggest all leaders tend to have. Another way to look at these is through the lens of what Myles Downey (2004) calls the coaching continuum. We have adapted the version below to show where we think type two (mentoring) and type three (coaching) fit within his model.

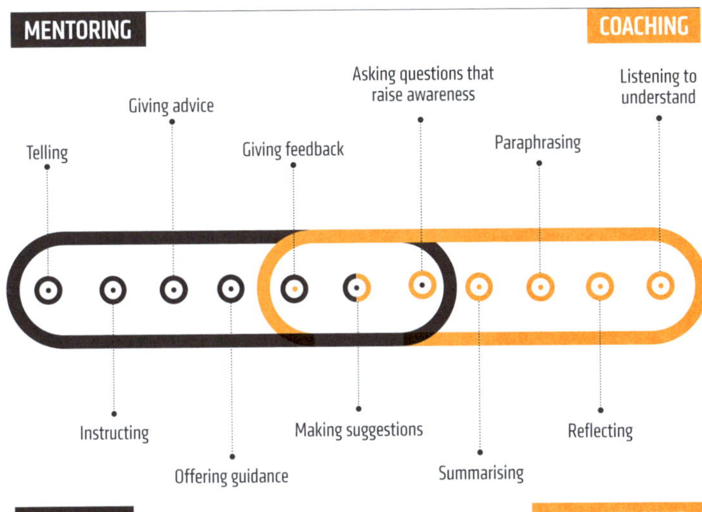

THE COACHING CONTINUUM
ADAPTED FROM MYLES DOWNEY (2004)

In keeping with the *ask first* approach, one should aspire to begin at the right of the model and only move left along the continuum when you judge it necessary. With inexperienced colleagues, taking the time to teach or show them how to do something is great, but it isn't a habit you want to form or you run the risk of forgetting to lead.

Productive conversations

Having productive conversations with colleagues isn't just about having the right type of conversation, there is also something important about the way these conversations are conducted. Put it bluntly, what's it like *talking to you*? Below are some key features that can really help conversations be more effective.

Having productive conversations with colleagues isn't just about having the right type of conversation

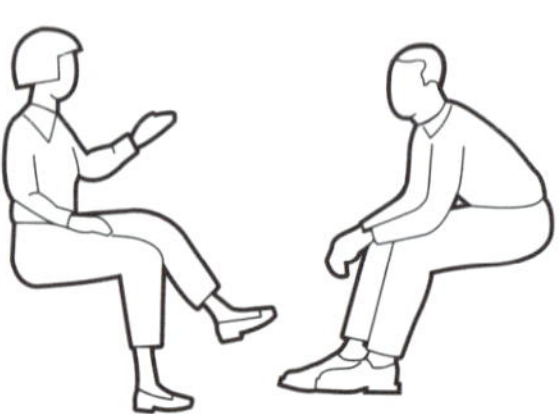

- ✓ Build rapport and empathy
- ✓ Show humility
- ✓ Listen and playback
- ✓ Be curious not judging

- ✓ Give your full attention and time
- ✓ Ask before you tell or model
- ✓ Be challenging but supportive
- ✓ Be positive and empowering

Curious, not judging

To pick up on one area from this table, ensuring you are curious, not judging can make a real difference to what it's like to talk with you. You will know how it feels when someone you are talking to appears to be judging either you or what you are saying, we typically go into a more defensive mode and seek to protect our position. I am not saying that sometimes this isn't appropriate, but if this is your habit, you probably aren't going to help colleagues learn and grow as well as you might. Of course, there are times when a completely different type of very judgmental conversation is required, and Chapter 16 focuses on how to have these often difficult conversations.

The importance of listening and playing back

As David Hockney reminds us, 'Listening is a positive act. You have to put yourself out to do it'. Even when you have developed the habit of asking great questions, if you don't listen actively, you will be missing the opportunity to be even more effective. It is not about being soft. Listening to colleagues can give you important information about what is really happening on the ground, it provides room for your team to grow and develop their thinking and is more likely to lead to distributed and sustainable leadership. Henry Ford said: 'If there is any great secret of success in life, it lies in the ability to put yourself in the other person's place and to see things from his point of view.'

DAVID HOCKNEY

Listening is a positive act.
You have to put yourself out to do it

How far do you listen beyond the words for what is really behind a conversation, what isn't being said?

The first thing about listening is that it is active not passive. When done well, listening gives you information about a situation or individual, and leads you towards greater insight, awareness and learning. You might see a different perspective or clarify your thinking. Active listening relies on good questioning. By structuring your questions, you can lead someone through a thinking process or suggest new ways of approaching a problem. How well do you tend to structure your questions at the moment? Are they leading or open? Do they provide enough space for the other person to reflect?

You can also listen and pick up information that goes beyond the words being used. You can 'listen' for emotion, body language, tone of voice, speed of talking and clarity of thinking. By listening actively for these, you can discern a great deal about the other person's frame of mind, emotional state and the purpose of the conversation. Often the words someone is using do not reflect what they really mean or want to say. How far do you listen beyond the words for what is really behind a conversation, what isn't being said?

Nancy Kline (2009) talks about creating a 'thinking environment' for a person by listening to them in what she calls a 'generative' way with a totally positive disposition towards the individual. It starts with a basic 'What do you think and what are your thoughts?' When the person flags, the questioner asks: 'And what else are you thinking?' Giving someone space and time to think is liberating for them and can lead to them solving their own issues in an environment set by the coach. Nancy's most recent book, *More Time to Think* is well worth a read.

NANCY KLINE

How to show you are listening

Others are more likely to share if they feel you are listening to them, and that your listening will result in some action or change. To a certain extent the relevance of your questions will demonstrate that you are listening, but other techniques you can use include reflecting back the words someone has used or making statements showing you understand their emotions. Your body language and tone of voice can mirror the non-verbal signals they are giving, so if they are angry you might choose to change your body language and tone of voice be less confrontational; if they are upset you might again change them to elicit a different response. Having an awareness of the differences in communication and processing styles between you and the person you are communicating with is essential. To be an effective listener, it's important to be calm and create enough space to listen and absorb what is being said. *If you are too busy talking and preparing what you will say next, how will you know what is really being said to you?* This skill of being able to think and listen at the same time is an important one to develop.

Four levels of listening

The importance of actively listening is summarised well in Julie Starr's *Four Levels of listening* model. The further down the model you go the better your listening is and the more productive the outcomes.

LEVEL	WHEN	WHAT OTHER PERSON THINKS
1 Attending	Eye contact and body language show interest	This person wants to listen to me
2 Accurate listening	Above — plus accurate paraphrasing of what the other says	This person hears and understands what I am talking about
3 Empathetic listening	All of above — plus matching non-verbal cues with metaphor use and own feelings	This person knows what it feels like to be in my situation
4 Generative empathetic listening	All of above — plus the ability to use intuition and feelings to connect more fully and deeply with the other person's situation	This person helps me to hear myself more fully than I can by myself, without telling me what to do, is helping me to find my own way

To summarise the key content in this chapter, one need look no further than the excellent definition of coaching from Christian van Nieuwerburgh in his great book *An Introduction to Coaching Skills* (2017) which contains all the elements discussed so far:

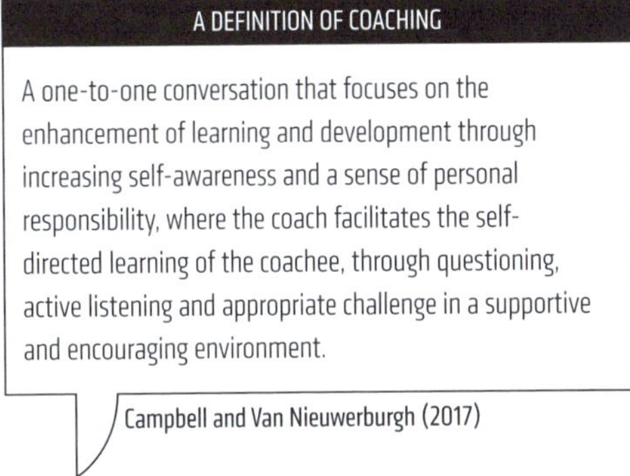

Structuring your coaching conversations using BASIC

So you have the right overall approach to your coaching conversations, but how can they be structured? At *Honk!* we have developed an approach known as the BASIC coaching model.

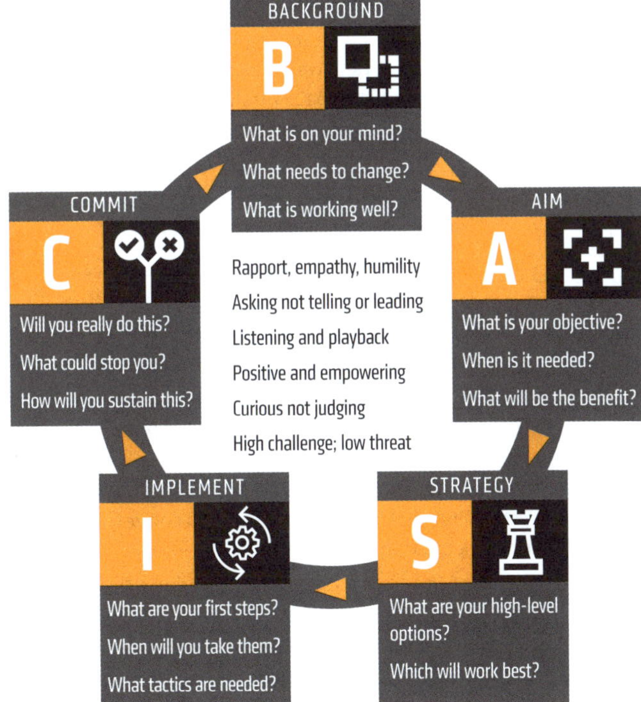

By taking time to understand the **background** to a situation, both you and your colleague have the chance to reflect on the current context.

This can have the benefit of allowing someone to let off steam if this is needed. It also allows the person to start to organise their thoughts and enable you to ask questions based on what you are hearing that can build rapport.

If colleagues are clear about the benefits a change will bring, this really helps to increase the chances of it actually happening

You are then ready to help colleagues focus on the solution, **aim** or goal they want to achieve. Getting them to frame their goal as precisely as possible can really help. It can also be helpful to ask what the benefit of achieving the aim will be. If colleagues are clear about the benefits a change will bring, this really helps to increase the chances of it actually happening. So too can framing an aim in the future perfect tense – the sense that by a certain date they *will* have achieved their aim, rather than it being something they *will do*. When setting objectives, Fergal would always get his direct reports to 'stand on' a particular date in the future, as if it were the finishing line, and look back on the journey behind them. What happened? What did they do to ensure they made it to the line?

A very powerful question at this point can just be 'what else?'

Once the aim is clear, you can then focus on their high level options or their **strategy**. This part of the conversation is about exploring the possible ways of achieving their aim. It is sometimes useful to spend a bit more time on the background at this point, particularly focusing on the current positives as well as the barriers they need to overcome to help them find solutions. A very powerful question at this point can just be 'what else?' It's amazing what such a simple enquiry can elicit from colleagues. We often find that it is at this point in a conversation that a really helpful new idea or strategy can emerge.

The next stage is to fine tune the strategies into actions that colleagues are going to **implement** and, in particular, their very next steps. Pinning these down to specific dates and even times can help them avoid procrastination. Depending on the context, this part of the conversation may also involve sketching out a rough plan of action to follow after that. Very often however, just getting someone started on a next step can be all that's needed.

Finally, one usually needs to make sure that whatever is going to happen or change, your colleague is going to **commit** to make it happen, both in the short and longer term. Asking how colleagues will sustain whatever they have decided to do can really make them focus on developing useful habits that will ensure ongoing benefit from the change.

On the subject of habits, in the **centre** of the BASIC model are some of the coaching habits we explored earlier that can help these conversations go well. In particular, keeping a neutral or curious demeanour can be really helpful. If you avoid your questions feeling like an interrogation, colleagues will quickly feel at ease and more able to say what they are really thinking about something, rather than trying to come up with what they think you want to hear. Building rapport in this manner and empowering others to own their next steps in a positive fashion is a powerful way to build trust, confidence and competence in others. Moreover, it means any solutions that emerge will be much more likely to happen because your colleague truly believes in them.

ANY SOLUTIONS THAT EMERGE WILL BE MUCH MORE LIKELY TO HAPPEN BECAUSE YOUR COLLEAGUE TRULY BELIEVES IN THEM

Nudges

- How good are you at using the range of techniques outlined in the coaching spectrum?

- Do you tend to be curious, not judging?

- How good a listener are you? How do others know?

- Do you understand the use of body language?

- Do you use a coaching model to help you structure your coaching conversations?

- Might the BASIC coaching model be useful in your context?

Final thoughts

Excellence is an art won by training and habituation. We do not act rightly because we have virtue or excellence, but we rather have those because we have acted rightly. We are what we repeatedly do. Excellence, then, is not an act but a habit.

ARISTOTLE

Born 384 BCE, Aristotle was a Greek philosopher and scientist and one of the greatest intellectual figures of Western history. He was the author of a philosophical and scientific system that became the framework and vehicle of Christian Scholasticism and medieval Islamic philosophy. Many of his concepts remain embedded in Western thinking today.

At *Honk!* we have become increasingly convinced that it is the development of the right leadership habits that makes the biggest difference to the effective leadership of organisations. Every day we visit work places where we have the privilege to reflect on what leaders are up to on a routine basis.

This final part of the book is our attempt to summarise what we think are, if you asked us to choose from everything in the previous chapters, the top six habits that leaders might prioritise. While being influenced by research and evidence, this is more of a personal view of what seems to us to represent the habits demonstrated by the most successful leaders at all levels within both private and public sectors across a wide range of organisations and companies.

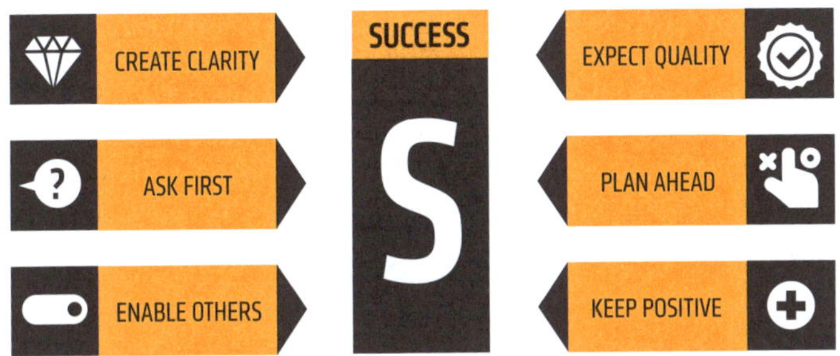

Great leaders create clarity

Both individual colleagues and teams will be more motivated if they
know what is expected of them and you give them the chance to get
good at stuff. There is nothing worse for staff than not being clear
about 'the way we do things around here'. Are you clear about those
things you expect to be done uniformly and those where there is scope
to work more flexibly within a set of guiding principles? Do you take
every opportunity to reinforce clarity and check for understanding? It's
the first step in creating consistent outcomes for staff, customers and
stakeholders.

Are you clear about those things you expect
to be done uniformly and those where there
is scope to work more flexibly

Great leaders expect quality

Selling and modelling an inspiring vision for the future is a
powerful motivator for employees. If you have the habit of taking
every opportunity to reinforce this vision through your everyday
conversations, you will be aware of the powerful effect this can have,
especially if you are always on the lookout to celebrate and highlight
when colleagues are demonstrating what these expectations look like.
How well do you reinforce the highest expectations of yourself and
everyone else in every conversation you have?

Great leaders plan ahead

Stepping off the dance floor and looking down from the balcony is
a vital habit for any leader. Seeing this bigger picture enables you to

take a longer term view to planning and strategy. It also means you can create a powerful culture, because implementation is properly thought through and not rushed. There is often nothing your staff will hate more – and therefore buy into less – than a last minute and rushed new idea. Finally, good planning forces good prioritisation which, with well-being becoming increasingly important, has to be a good thing.

Good planning forces good prioritisation

Great leaders enable others

Leading is all about bringing out the best in others and helping them to lead with you on your journey together. This involves building trust, capacity and confidence in those around you. It also means developing the habit of *letting go*. Some leaders find this habit harder to develop than almost any other; the knowledge that you can quite often do something faster and better than a busy colleague is often a barrier to giving them opportunities. How good are you at empowering your staff, not only by delegating projects but also by allowing them to make decisions when working on them?

Leading is all about bringing out the best in others and helping them to lead with you

Great leaders keep it positive

Whatever your own thoughts and emotions, keeping a focus on the positive – however hard this may sometimes be – can make a real difference to how staff are feeling. Great leaders have the habit of focusing on how far you have come and the positive future you are headed to, creating a more can-do culture and a more optimistic climate. Focusing on the problems you currently face does exactly the opposite. That's not to say these leaders ignore the challenges, it just means they acknowledge them and then focus on what's to be done and the benefit of doing it.

Great leaders have the habit of focusing on how far you
have come and the positive future you are headed to

Great leaders *ask first*

The one leadership habit we think underpins pretty much everything
great leaders do is that of *asking first*. If you want to understand yourself
and your context better, you need to ask questions of yourself, others
and your context, and you need to interrogate the data you have at your
disposal. Only by doing this are you in a position to identify what you
need to make your priorities for action. And only then can you decide
on how you will implement these priorities: your leadership approach.
The everyday habit is about asking questions at the start of most
conversations, rather than straightaway giving advice or taking on a job
yourself. This also has the advantage of making colleagues feel listened
to, valued and cared for.

The everyday habit is about asking questions
at the start of most conversations

And finally ...

Leadership is a remarkable privilege whatever your role. What you do
and how you do it has the potential to transform lives and make a real
difference, whether you are working in the public sector, a business or
a charity. With all its ups and downs, leading in any organisation can be
a terrifically rewarding job. If you can step back from time to time and
reflect on some of the ideas we have offered in this book, we hope you
will feel inspired to be even better at bringing out the best in others. Do
this with professionalism, determination, transparency and drive and
we are sure you will see the difference you can make.

Leading in any organisation can be a
terrifically rewarding job

Throughout this book our aim has been to offer practical tools you can try out in your organisation, all underpinned by tried and tested theoretical frameworks, topped off with some inspirational tales from real people who have made a difference. Throughout this process, we have tried to take the complex and make it simple without making it simplistic.

But more than that, we hope we have inspired you in the next stage of your personal leadership journey, wherever that may take you, and with whomever you may lead. May we wish you all success in your leadership roles, now and in the future.

And remember, when you Honk! make sure it's positive and encouraging!

Key references

Ancona, D., Malone, T.W., Orlikowski, W.J., and Senge, P.M. (2007) In praise of the incomplete leader. *Harvard Business Review* February 2007 (2) pp 109-118. Available at https://hbr.org/2007/02/in-praise-of-the-incomplete-leader

Black, P. and Wiliam, D. (1998) Inside the Black Box: Raising Standards Through Classroom Assessment. *Phi Delta Kappan* 80 (2) pp 139–144, 146–148.

Bambrick-Santoyo, P. (2012) *Leverage Leadership: a practical guide to building exceptional schools.* San Francisco: Jossey-Bass.

Brighouse, T. (2007) *How successful head teachers survive and thrive.* Abingdon: RM Publications.

Brighouse, T. and Woods, D. (2008) *What makes a good school now?* London: Network Continuum.

Campbell, A. (2015) *Winners: And how they succeed.* London: Hutchinson.

Van Nieuwerburgh, C. (2017) *An Introduction to Coaching Skills.* London: Sage.

Clough, P. and Strycharczyk, D. (2012) *Developing Mental Toughness: Improving Performance, Wellbeing and Positive Behaviour in Others.* London: Kogan Page.

Coffield, F., Moseley, D., Hall, E., and Ecclestone, K. (2004) *Learning styles and pedagogy in post-16 learning. A systematic and critical review.* London: Learning and Skills Research Centre.

Collins, J. (2001) *Good to great.* New York: Collins Business.

Corporate Leadership Council (2004) *Driving Performance and Retention Through Employee Engagement.* Available at: http://cwfl.usc.edu/assets/pdf/Employee%20engagement.pdf

Covey, S. (2008) *The speed of trust. One thing that changes everything.* London: Simon and Schuster.

Covey, S. (2004) *The 7 habits of highly effective people.* London: Simon and Schuster.

Department for Education (2016) *Expert group report on continuing professional development*. London: The Stationary Office.

Department for Education (2016) *Standard for teachers' professional development*. London: The Stationary Office.

Downey, M. (2003) *Effective Coaching: Lessons from the Coach's Coach*. London: Texere Publishing.

Drucker, P. (2007) *Essential Drucker: management, the individual and society*. New York: Routledge.

Dudley, P. (2014) *Lesson study: professional learning for our time*. New York: Routledge.

Dweck, C. (2012) *Mindset: How You Can Fulfil Your Potential*. New York: Ballantine Books.

Education Endowment Foundation (2014) *Teaching and Learning Toolkit*.
Available at: https://educationendowmentfoundation.org.uk/evidence-summaries/teaching-learning-toolkit

Education Endowment Foundation (2015) *Making the best use of teaching assistants*. Available at:
https://educationendowmentfoundation.org.uk/tools/making-best-use-of-teaching-assistants/guidance-report/

Fullan, M. (2001) *Leading the culture of change*. San Francisco: Jossey-Bass.

Fullan, M. (2008) *The six secrets of change*. San Francisco: Jossey-Bass.

Gawande, A. (2011) *The Checklist Manifesto: How to Get Things Right*. New York: Henry Holt.

Goleman, D., Boyatzis, R.E. and McKee, A. (2002) *The new leaders*. London: Little, Brown.

Goleman, D. (2000) Leadership that gets results. *Harvard Business Review* March-April 2000 (03) pp 78-90.
Available at: https://hbr.org/2000/03/leadership-that-gets-results

Goleman, D. (1995) *Emotional Intelligence: Why it Can Matter More Than IQ*. London: Bloomsbury.

Growth Coaching International (2016) Available at: www.growthcoaching.com.au/the-growth-approach.html

Heifetz, R. and Linsky, M. (2002) *Leadership on the Line: Staying Alive through the Dangers of Leading*. Boston: Harvard Business School Press.

Handy, C. (1997) *The hungry spirit*. London: Hutchinson.

Hattie, J. (2009) *Visible Learning: A Synthesis of Over 800 Meta-Analyses Relating to Achievement*. New York: Routledge.

Hargreaves, D. (2011) *Leading a self-improving school system: towards maturity*. NCSL. Available at: www.gov.uk/government/publications/a-self-improving-school-system-towards-maturity

Hay Group (2007) *Rush to the top: Accelerating the development of leaders in schools*. Available at: www.haygroup.com/downloads/uk/Rush_to_the_Top_low_res.pdf

House of Commons Education Committee (2017) *Multi-academy trusts*
Education Select Committee Report. Available at: https://publications.parliament.uk/pa/cm201617/cmselect/cmeduc/204/204.pdf

Jones, G. (2016) *Evidence Based Management, The Basic Principles*.
Amsterdam: The Centre for Evidence Based Management.

Kahneman, D. (2012) *Thinking, fast and slow*. London: Penguin.

Katzenbach, J.R. and Smith, D.K. (2003) *The Wisdom of Teams: Creating the High-Performance Organization*. Boston: Harvard Business School Press.

Kilmann, R. (1994) *Producing useful knowledge for organisations*. San Francisco: Jossey-Bass.

Kline, N. (2009) *More Time to Think*. London: Ward Lock.

Knoster, T., Villa R. and Thousand, J. (2000) *A framework for thinking about systems change*. Baltimore: Paul H. Brookes Publishing Co.

Koch, R. (1998) The 80/20 *Principle: The Secret of Achieving More with Less*. New York: Doubleday.

Kotter, J.P. (1996) *Leading change*. Boston: Harvard Business Review Press.

Kübler-Ross, E. (1969) *On death and dying*. New York: Scribner.

Leithwood, K., Day, C., Sammons, P., Harris, A. and Hopkins, D. (2006) *Seven strong claims about successful school leadership*. Nottingham: National College for School Leadership.

Lencioni, P.M. (2002) *The five dysfunctions of a team; a leadership fable*. San Francisco: Jossey-Bass.

Lencioni, P.M. (2012) *The Advantage*. San Francisco: Jossey-Bass.

Luft, J. and Ingham, H. (1955) *The Johari window, a graphic model of interpersonal awareness.* Los Angeles: University of California.

Matthews, P. (2009) *Twelve outstanding secondary schools.* Ofsted. Available at: http://dera.ioe.ac.uk/11232/

Matthews, P. (2017) The power of incremental coaching – improving teacher quality. *Professional Development Today* 19 (1).

McGregor, D. (1960) *The Human Side of Enterprise.* New York: McGraw-Hill.

Mehrabian, A. (1972) *Nonverbal Communication.* New Brunswick: Aldine Transaction.

Muijs, D. and Reynolds, D. (2011) *Effective Teaching: Evidence and Practice.* London: Sage.

National Governors' Association (2015) *A Framework for Governance.* Available at: www.nga.org.uk/Services/Clerking-Matters/Clerk-to-governors/Framework-for-Governance.aspx

NCSL (2003) *Heart of the matter: a practical guide to what middle leaders can do to improve learning in secondary schools.* Available at: http://webarchive.nationalarchives.gov.uk/tna/20140701125459/http:/nationalcollege.org.uk/docinfo?id=17209&filename=heart-of-the-matter.pdf

NCSL (2004) *A model of school leadership in challenging urban environments.* Available at: http://dera.ioe.ac.uk/5276/7/download_id%3D17300%26filename%3Dmodel-of-school-leadership-in-challenging-urban-environments_Redacted.pdf

Pendleton, D. and Furnham, A. (2012) *Leadership: all you need to know.* Basingstoke: Palgrave Macmillan.

Pink, D.H. (2011) *Drive: the surprising truth about what motivates us.* New York: Riverhead Books.

Radcliffe, S. (2012) *Leadership: plain and simple.* (2nd ed.) Edinburgh: Pearson.

Reynolds, D. (2004) *Within-school variation: its extent and causes.* Available at: www.highreliabilityschools.co.uk/_resources/files/downloads/within-school-variation/dr2004a1.pdf

Robertson Cooper (2018) *The i-resilience report.* Available at: www.robertsoncooper.com/

Robinson, V. (2011) *Pupil centred leadership.* San Francisco: Jossey-Bass.

Scott, K. (2017) *Radical Candor*. New York: St Martin's Press.

Scott, S. (2003) *Fierce conversations*. London: Piatkus.

Sherrington, T. (2017) Blogs on workload. Available at: https://teacherhead.com/tag/workload/

Sinek, S. (2011) *Start with why. How great leaders inspire everyone to take action*. New York: Penguin.

Starr, J. (2002) *The coaching manual*. London: Pearson.

Strong, M., Gargani, J. and Hacifazlioğluet, O. (2011) Do we know a successful teacher when we see one? Experiments in the identification of successful teachers. *Journal of Teacher Education* 62 (4) pp 367-382. Available at http://journals.sagepub.com/doi/abs/10.1177/0022487110390221

Tuckman, B. (1965) Developmental sequence in small groups. *Psychological Bulletin* 63 (6) pp 384–99.

Ward, S. (2009) *Time management types*. Available at: http://sbinfocanada.about.com/cs/timemanagement/a/timetypes.htm

Watkins, M. (2003) *The first 90 days*. Boston: Harvard Business Review Press.

Whitmore, J. (2009) *Coaching for performance GROWing Human Potential and Purpose – the Principles and Practice of Coaching and Leadership*. (4th ed.) London: Nicholas Brealy.

Wiliam, D. (2015) The research delusion. *Times Educational Supplement*, 10 April 2015.

Yerkes, R.M. and Dodson, J.D. (1908) The relation of strength of stimulus to rapidity of habit-formation. *Journal of Comparative Neurology and Psychology* 18 (5) 99 459-482. Available at: www.viriya.net/jabref/the_relation_of_strength_of_stimulus_to_rapidity_of_habit-formation.pdf